100 Ideas for Secondary Teachers

Outstanding Mathematics Lessons

Other titles in the 100 Ideas for Secondary Teachers series:

100 Ideas for Secondary Teachers

Outstanding Mathematics Lessons

Mike Ollerton

B L O O M S B U R Y

LONDON • NEW DELHI • NEW YORK • SYDNEY

Bloomsbury Education

An imprint of Bloomsbury Publishing Plc

50 Bedford Square
London
WC1B 3DP
UK

1385 Broadway
New York
NY 10018
USA

www.bloomsbury.com

Published 2014

British Library Cataloguing-in-Publication Data
A catalogue record for this book is available from the British Library.

ISBN: PB: 9781408194874
ePub: 9781408194881
ePDF: 9781472900401

Library of Congress Cataloging-in-Publication Data
A catalog record for this book is available from the Library of Congress.

10 9 8 7 6 5 4 3 2 1

Typeset by Newgen Knowledge Works (P) Ltd., Chennai, India
Printed and bound by CPI Group (UK) Ltd, Croydon, CR0 4YY

This book is produced using paper that is made from wood grown
in managed, sustainable forests. It is natural, renewable and
recyclable. The logging and manufacturing processes conform
to the environmental regulations of the country of origin.

To view more of our titles please visit www.bloomsbury.com

Contents

Acknowledgements

Idea 7: Opening quote from www.ted.com/talks/ken_robinson_says_schools_kill_creativity

Idea 7: Idea adapted from a session at the Association of Teachers of Mathematics conference, Swansea University, in 2009, led by Anne Watson and Nichola Clarke.

Idea 10: With thanks to Jason Doucette, www.jasondoucette.com/worldrecords.html#196, for the palindromic solution to 89.

Idea 12: This problem appears in the Association of Teachers of Mathematics publication: *Points of Departure 3*. A write-up of this problem from 1989 by David Sutcliffe, a then Year 10 student, appears in Mathematics Teaching 127, pp 26–27.

Idea 15: A fuller explanation is in Mathematics Teaching (MT232) pp 29–30.

Idea 20: I have John Mason to thank for this task; he introduced it to me when I was studying with the Open University many years ago.

Idea 25: With thanks to Daniela Vasile, Head of Mathematics, South Island School, Hong Kong for the second bonus idea.

Idea 34: I first met this problem in: *Starting Points* (1972) by Banwell, Saunders and Tahta pp 44–47. If you can get hold of a copy of this seminal text, never lend it out!

Idea 40: My thanks goes to Peter Hampson, a former headteacher.

Idea 53: The number of possible convex polygons is according to an article by Jean Sauvy in *Mathematics Teaching* 114, March 1986.

Idea 57: Wells, D., (1991) *The Penguin Dictionary of Curious and Interesting Geometry*, London, Penguin.

Idea 58: Opening quote from Mason, J., with Burton, L., & Stacey, K., (1985) Thinking mathematically, Wokingham, Addison-Wesley

Idea 70: Opening quote from Wigley *Models for Teaching Mathematics* (1992, p6).

Idea 71: Opening quote from French, *Teaching and Learning Geometry*, Continuum (2004, p17).

Idea 72: Association of Teachers of Mathematics, www.atm.org.uk

Idea 73: Opening quote from Cundy and Rollett, *Mathematical Models*, Tarquin Publications (1981, p70).

Idea 91: Ollerton, M., and Watson, A., (2001) *Inclusive Mathematics 11–18*, London, Continuum.

Introduction

The following quotation by Pennac describes one of his mathematics teachers.

It's a matter of luck, and no thanks to the greatness of the institution, if a pupil, from time to time, meets a mathematics teacher who is enthusiastic enough to consider mathematics in their own right. Imparting maths as if they were Fine Arts, the teacher inspires a love for them by virtue of his (her) own vitality, and thanks to him (her) effort is turned into pleasure. It's the prerogative of living beings to inspire a love for life, even in the form of a quadratic equation.

Pennac, D., (1994) *Reads like a novel*, London, Quartet Books.

I offer it because I feel it is both profound and humbling and because it captures my own love for mathematics and the journey of how I learnt to teach it in ways which helps learners to make sense of this fascinating and highly complex discipline.

How anyone teaches mathematics, in ways which helps their students become confident learners, so they are able to appreciate the value and the purposes of mathematics is indeed a complex business and whilst I am not great fan of the existing inspection system I could not help but value the following: 'Nobody – government, local authorities or Ofsted – is telling teachers how they should teach.' (Sir Michael Wilshaw, Her Majesty's Chief Inspector, North of England Education Conference, 15 January 2014)

The idea that somewhere 'out there' has an elixir brewed from a secret formula which, if only we knew what it was, we could all teach outstanding lessons is nonsensical. We all know those lessons we have taught which have gone really well with one class yet have gone down like a lead balloon with another. We also know of teachers who always seem to have that 'knack' of working with their students in positive, interesting ways...if only we could bottle 'it'. But of course even 'those' teachers have their off-days.

Given the complexities and the vast differences between one teacher's outstanding practice and another's I seek not to offer my own formulae; I am reminded of a story from *The exploits of the incomparable Mulla Nasrudin* by Idries Shah which I paraphrase as follows: Mulla Nasrudin has bought himself a piece of liver from the local market and is returning to his house to cook it for supper. Having spotted the liver in Nasrudin's open basket, a crow flies down, takes the liver in its beak and flies off. Not to be outdone Nasrudin shakes his stick at the bird and shouts: 'You might have my liver but you don't have my recipe!' Likewise I can offer ideas which you might be interested in thinking about and using in your classrooms but applying your own teaching style, methods and approaches. Furthermore, I am not for one moment suggesting what I have to offer is either unique or of my own 'invention'. I have invented very few ideas and even those I may have thought were 'mine', were probably a subconscious retrieval or an adaptation of an idea I met through discussion with a colleague, at a conference or something I had read. Who knows the many different ways we learn?

It is upon these bases I offer the ideas in this book together with some structural 'stuff' in this introduction which I find helps my learners and at the same time enhances my practice. Indeed, only this week, I engaged with someone in a professional development session where I consciously chose not to suggest 'my' way was better the other person's; the impact of which, I believed, had a far more purposeful impact upon everyone in the group than had I entered into a two-way argument.

I also offer some thoughts on planning, use of equipment and the use of problem solving, whilst acknowledging there are always pros and cons; the only person who can make a valid decision about why, how or when to employ them is the class teacher. If you like, therefore, here are my ingredients without the recipes; they are only any use in my classroom depending upon how and when I choose to use them. Thus read on with caution!

Paired talk
Pros: This enables students to discuss something they know and rehearse some answers to an 'open' question (for example, discuss for two minutes everything you know about the number 6). Asking each pair to subsequently say one thing they have discussed and the teacher précising these responses on the board can lead to an interesting array of information. The feedback provides the teacher with assessment opportunities which, in turn, can lead to further questions to develop a pair of students' responses.

Cons: In the main I have found this a really powerful strategy. However, if in five or six daily lessons, every child experiences the paired talk strategy they might soon get bored.

Use of equipment
Pros: Providing students with manipulatives such as geoboards, pegboards, linking cubes, dominoes, dice, paper for paper folding etc can provide them with first-hand experiences to make sense of mathematical concepts.

Cons: Equipment is, of course, not imbued with magical powers and unless students become used to working with equipment in their mathematics lessons, some may well see this as an opportunity or a tool with which to misbehave. Developing a culture of students using manipulatives is something which needs to be worked on carefully and determinedly; thinking through how and why one may wish students to use a geoboard is a key part of the planning process.

The importance of problem solving

In support of problem solving as a way to engage students in their learning of mathematics I offer the following three quotes:

'I like the way you discover things as you go along.' Nick Park, Desert Island Discs BBC Radio 4, 12 December 2010

'It's not easy, being clever, is it? You look at the world and you connect things, random things.' David Tennant, Dr Who, Series 4, episode 4

'Problem solving, discussion and investigation are seen as integral to learning mathematics.' Ofsted 'Outstanding' Criteria 2012

Pros: I believe learners are naturally curious and that mathematics has only been constructed in order to a) solve problems and b) make sense of the physical, social, intellectual and emotional world in which we live. Teaching mathematics, therefore, through the medium of problem solving is, essential

Cons: Working investigationally and exploring structures within mathematics needs to be supported by two further processes. These are a) practice and consolidation of routines and methods and b) students knowing **why** they are being asked to solve problems. Furthermore, anticipating and being prepared to answer questions from students such as: 'Is this going to be on the exam?' or 'Why are we doing this?' is important and sometimes necessary.

Some of the 'best' problems, in my opinion, are those which offer students a sense of exploration whilst at the same time require them to practise skills in order to make in-roads in a problem. With this in mind I offer readers 100 ideas, to do with as you so choose.

We know when we have taught an outstanding lesson though this is less about our 'performance' and more about students' engagement. Such engagement occurs as a consequence of the quality and accessibility of the task we offer students which, in turn, is about spending more time planning and preparing lessons. I hope this book will support teachers of mathematics with such planning and preparation.

Mike Ollerton
April 2014

How to use this book

This book includes quick, easy, practical ideas for you to dip in and out of, to support you in teaching secondary maths.

Each idea includes:

- A catchy title, easy to refer to and share with your colleagues.
- A quote from a teacher or student describing their experiences of the idea that follows or a problem they may have had that using the idea solves.
- A summary of the idea in bold, making it easy to flick through the book and identify an idea you want to use at a glance.
- A step-by-step guide to implementing the idea.

Each idea also includes one or more of the following:

Teaching tip

Some extra advice on how or how not to run the activity or put the strategy into practice.

Taking it further

Ideas and advice for how to extend the idea or develop it further.

Bonus idea ★

There are 32 bonus ideas in this book that are extra exciting and extra original.

Online resources also accompany this book. When the link to the resource is referenced in the book, logon to www.bloomsbury.com/100ideas-maths to find the extra resources, catalogued under the relevant idea number.

Share how you use these ideas in the classroom and find out what other teachers have done using **#100ideas.**

Number puzzles

Part 1

Exploring a 99 square

"Projecting an image of a 99 square on the board and asking students to discuss will result in lots of really interesting observations and trigger some great conversations."

The 99 square is becoming a preferred resource to the 100 square because it naturally includes the all-important value of zero. Exploring patterns on such a number grid will enhance students' understanding of the way numbers are connected.

A 99 square is a 10 by 10 grid containing the numbers from 0 to 9 in the bottom row, 10 to 19 in the next row up, and so on (see the online resources for an example). Asking students to find the numerical functions that describe movements around the number board helps to emphasise the relationships between the numbers. For example starting at any number (n) and moving one space to the right takes us to $n + 1$, so the function is +1. Similarly moving one space up produces the function +10 ($n + 10$). What functions describe movements of one space downwards (D), and one space left (L)?

Once the basic movements have been mastered, introduce combinations of movements. For example, the function created for U followed by R (or UR) is +10 followed by +1 or +11 What about DR? What about 2R + 3U? Students can then try to answer these questions without adding every number separately.

- What do the numbers on the bottom row sum to?
- What about the numbers on the next row up?
- What do the numbers in the column ending in the digit 4 sum to?
- What is the sum of the numbers in the diagonal from 0 to 99? From 9 to 91?

A place value exploration

"The concept of place value underpins almost everything else that we teach in mathematics!"

This idea lets students explore place value to the right of the decimal point using a grid upon which they place numbers to create different values.

Use a two column grid with one column for units, and one for tenths. Ensure decimal points are clearly marked on the line between the columns. Fill in the first column for the students with 1 unit and 1 tenth. Have three rows with a 0 in each column, and a row for the total.

Ask the students to place the digits 1, 3 and 5 on any of the six zeros and find the total. The idea is to find out how many different totals can be formed. Develop the task by asking the students to:

- describe how they know they have found all the possible totals
- place the totals in order from smallest to largest
- place each result on a number line.

Suppose the grid consisted of three columns (either HTU or TU.t or U.th) and two rows of zeros; what different values can be gained using just two digits? What if the grid consisted of three columns and three rows using three digits?

Teaching tip

Key Stage 3 (KS3) students' understanding of place value cannot be taken for granted and their understanding of this concept needs to be carefully checked, worked on and developed. The initial task purposefully uses three numbers whose sum is less than 10. Seeing how students cope with values whose sum is greater than 10 will be a useful development.

Taking it further

Ask students to find the positive difference between adjacent pairs of totals. What do all these differences total to? Repeat the idea with tenths and hundredths instead of units and tenths, using the same three numbers as before. Let the students choose three of their own digits and see what happens. Do two people achieve the same answers using the same three digits?

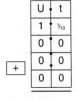

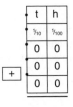

Consecutive sums

"My favourite way of introducing any idea is to draw upon students' natural sense of curiosity."

Consecutive sums provide students with insights into the properties of numbers. For example, prime numbers over 3 only ever have one consecutive sum; powers of 2 do not have any consecutive sums and triangular numbers over 3 have at least one consecutive sum.

Teaching tip

In order to analyse and classify numbers against their consecutive number sums, students will need a large collection of data. With this in mind, working in a group of, say, four may be useful to share out and check each other's work. The idea is to find all the consecutive sums for all the numbers up to, say, 50.

Bonus idea ★

Using and applying algebra is an important part of thinking mathematically as it lets students see how the structure of a mathematical puzzle works. The sum of any three consecutive numbers, algebraically, is $n + (n + 1) + (n + 2)$. Can the students use this to prove that the sum of any three consecutive numbers is always the middle number, $(n + 1)$, multiplied by 3?

Ask each pair of students to write down three consecutive numbers, all under 20, and add them together. Then ask a selection of pairs to reveal what their total is and watch their amazement when you announce the original three numbers they chose. The trick is to divide their total by 3; the answer will be the middle number of their consecutive set. So for example, if their total is 12 then their consecutive numbers must have been 3, 4 and 5 because $12 \div$ by $3 = 4$.

Then ask the students to try out the puzzle for themselves, and see if they are able to work out the trick. Once they have worked out the secret, try some of the following ideas:

- What happens if they add four consecutive numbers together?
- What about five consecutive numbers?
- Which numbers do not have any consecutive sums?
- Explore the sums of square numbers over 4.
- Explore the sums of prime numbers over 3.

Analysis of their results can lead to the idea of some numbers having more than one consecutive sum. The number 15, for example, has three consecutive sums which are $1 + 2 + 3 + 4 + 5$, $4 + 5 + 6$ and $7 + 8$.

Real life divisors

"I used this idea recently with a Year 7 class that I had 'borrowed' for a lesson."

This idea uses a people-maths strategy and is intended to help students make sense of divisors and prime numbers.

Invite five volunteers to perform the idea to the rest of the class, asking them to form two equal groups. Clearly this is not possible, but you can have great fun by pretending to be cross and telling them to do as you say! When they argue with you, saying it is impossible, ask them why.

When you finally 'give in' and admit that two equal groups can't be done, ask them to try to form three equal groups. Again this is clearly impossible.

Next, pose the question 'How many different groups *can* you form yourselves into?'.

Once you have discussed this with the students and (hopefully!) agreed that there are only two possible groupings (five groups of 1 and one group of 5), ask the students to draw a diagram to describe these two possibilities.

These drawings could be something such as:

Repeat the exercise with nine volunteers, then with different numbers. The students should come to realise that the number of groupings is the same as the number of divisors of the starting number.

The game of 5's and 3's

"It made my students' day when I gave them a set of dominoes to play with!"

This is a traditional domino game involving addition and division by 5 and 3.

Playing games with cards, dice and dominoes impacts upon children's mental arithmetic, strategic thinking and social development, as well as being fun! This game of dominoes is played in the normal way, by matching pairs of the same numbers, but after each turn the players add together the values appearing at either end. The points scored are equal to the result when the total is divided by 5 and/or 3. Below is the beginning of a game between two players A and B:

Player A plays the 5:4 domino. This scores 3 points, because $(5 + 4) \div 3 = 3$.

Player B adds 6:5 as shown. This scores 2 points, because $(6 + 4) \div 5 = 2$.

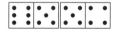

Player A adds 4:3 to the right-hand side as shown. This scores 3 points, because $(6 + 3) \div 3 = 3$. Player A's total is now 6 points.

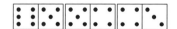

Player B now adds double 6, placed vertically next to the 6 as shown. In this case, both ends of the double 6 are counted in the total to make 6 + 6 + 3 = 15. Player B gets a total of 8 points, because 15 ÷ 5 = 3 and 15 ÷ 3 = 5.

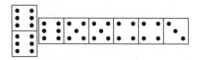

The game continues and the winner is the first person to score 121 points.

Taking it further

Explore patterns in different sizes of sets of dominoes and how many dominoes different set sizes contain. So in a 3-3 set there are 10 dominoes. Explore how many spots there are for different sized sets of dominoes.

Bonus idea ★

Domino magic

Ask students to choose any domino and decide which is the left-hand side and which is the right-hand side (if they choose a double then this of course does not matter). Then give them the following instructions:

- To the right-hand value add seven.
- Double the answer.
- Multiply the left-hand value by ten.
- Add this to your current total.
- Subtract the value of the right-hand value from your total.

By knowing the final total it is possible to predict the chosen domino. But how?

Divisor chains

"Helping children develop their arithmetical skills is fundamentally important; finding interesting tasks which aid this process is a worthy challenge."

This idea is an exploration of divisors to help students understand the structure of numbers.

This idea is about classifying numbers as follows:

- Deficient numbers – These are numbers whose divisor sum is less than the number itself. For example 10 is deficient as its divisor sum is 8.
- Perfect numbers – These are numbers whose divisor sum is equal to the number itself. There are only three such numbers less than 500: 6, 28 and 496.
- Abundant numbers – These are numbers whose divisor sum is greater than the number itself. For example 12 is abundant as its divisor sum is 16.

Ask the students to choose a number and write its divisors. Sum these divisors, apart from the number itself. For example, for the number 12 the divisors are 1, 2, 3, 4, 6 and 12, so excluding the 12 the sum is: $1 + 2 + 3 + 4 + 6 = 16$. 16 now becomes the second number in this divisor 'chain'.

Adding the divisors of 16 (apart from 16 itself) we have $1 + 2 + 4 + 8 = 15$. The chain continues as $(12 \rightarrow 16 \rightarrow 15 \rightarrow 9 \rightarrow 4 \rightarrow 3 \rightarrow 1)$.

Other starting numbers can subsequently be added to the diagram, for example:

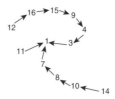

The dance of the divisors of 12

"I think math is very important, but so is dance. Children dance all the time if they're allowed to." (Sir Ken Robinson)

This idea is intended to provide students with opportunities to learn something about the structure of divisors while having a jolly time dancing.

Start by making a ring of 12 people, not holding hands, which represents 12 ones (or 1 x 12). When everybody hold hands they become one 12 (or 12 x 1).

12 people can form:

- two groups of six (6 x 2)
- six groups of two (2 x 6)
- four groups of three (3 x 4)
- three groups of four (4 x 3).

Each group may need someone to be 'scribe' (choreographer) to help keep a record of the types of groupings formed and reformed, and the order in which they are formed.

Invite students to find some music they can dance to. Encourage the groups to move away from the initial circle formation and plan a dance which is formed from 'smooth' transformations between different groups.

You can use Ceilidh or Country dance type moves so dancers interweave and interact in intricate patterns.

Teaching tip

Finding really 'real' contexts by contrast to pseudo 'real' contexts for learning mathematics is a worthy challenge. No textbook is required here to help students make sense of the concept of divisors. A group of students might want to create a dance for an open-evening or an assembly.

Taking it further

Students can make more complex groupings by, for example, having one person in the middle and five in a ring around the edge. The middle person of each group of six can do a little jig with each of the outer five, or the middle person might dance and swap places with an outside person, continuing until all six people in each group have been in the middle.

Doubling and doubling

"The students were shocked by how fast things grew when we doubled them."

An important concept is to see how quickly values increase by exponential growth.

Teaching tip

You may wish to use this as a non-calculator exercise so students can practise their mental arithmetic.

Give each student a penny, and challenge them to work out how many times they would need to double it to become a millionaire. How much faster would it be if they tripled it?

Give each student a sheet of paper and tell them to cut it in half. Place the two halves together; this is stage 1. Tear the stage 1 pile in half and place these two halves together. This is stage 2. Repeat this process a lot of times.

Taking it further

Explore the unit digits of sequences formed by doubling, tripling and so on. What about halving? Introduce the idea of 'exponents' and encourage students to find out what the word means.

Give the students this problem: if the paper was 0.01 cm thick, what would the height of the pile be after ten stages? What about 20 stages, or 50? What is the smallest number of stages they would need to make a pile the height of Mount Everest? You could link to other areas of the curriculum here by having students look up the height of different mountains or buildings, and work out how many stages are required for each one.

Dice games

"Virtual number games are alright . . . but there's nothing like the real thing – throwing 'real' dice is a different experience to seeing them appear on a screen."

Further opportunities for students to practise mental arithmetic skills using dice.

Here are two games that will let students practise their mental arithmetic while having fun with dice. These ideas could be used as one-off lessons, perhaps as a break between more developmental topics or units of work.

The six dice run

Throw six dice. The aim is to find runs, which must start from 1 and be at least two numbers in length. Score points by adding the numbers in each run. For example, with 5, 3, 6, 1, 2, 5 you can make a 1, 2, 3 run, which scores 6 points. With 2, 2, 6, 4, 3, 5 there is no score. With 3, 1, 6, 1, 2, 2 there are two runs: 1, 2 and 1, 2, 3 which score a total of $1 + 2 + 1 + 2 + 3 = 9$ points. Each person, in groups of threes or fours, might be given an agreed number of throws.

5 to 100

Throw five dice and use the values thrown as single digit numbers. The aim is to use all five numbers to make a total of 100. The numbers can be used in any order but only once each, and any of the four operations, as well as brackets, can be used as many times as needed. This could be a team effort, where different calculations score more points.

Palindromes

"My students thought I was crazy when I looked at the clock at 10:01 and said 'Ooh, that's a palindromic time!'"

The main point of this task is for students to collect and analyse data and seek to make conjectures about their data.

Start by explaining what a palindromic number is (a number that is the same whether read forwards or backwards). Then demonstrate the following process.

Choose a 2-digit number: **48**
Now reverse it: **84**
Now add the numbers: **132**

132 is not palindromic so continue by reversing and adding: 132 + 231 = 363. 363 is palindromic, so stop here.

The number 48 takes two stages (two additions) to become palindromic.

Now ask students to choose their own 2-digit numbers and see how many stages they need to make each one palindromic. What different palindromic answers are produced? After a while, collect all the answers and make a list of the starting numbers that give the same palindromic answers.

Number stories

"I chose the number 45 because I had recently seen my best 45 minutes of football watching Liverpool score three goals!"

The idea is to find facts about a number, which you could call 'the number of the week'.

Give the students a number, for example 45. Challenge the students to come up with questions and answers involving the number. The more interesting, the better!

Some examples are:

- What compass direction has a bearing of 045°?
- 45 is the sum of two squares; what are they?
- 45 is the difference of two squares; what are they?
- 45 is a triangular number; which one?
- What are the prime factors of 45?
- 45 is palindromic in base 2; what is this value?

Playing around with numbers in different bases is useful to hone students' number skills and help them to appreciate the powers of numbers. Connecting this to palindromes in different bases adds another layer for exploration.

Teaching tip

This activity could easily lead to groups producing posters of everything they know about the given number. Do this in the final 15 or so minutes of a lesson to create a sense of urgency.

Taking it further

Students could be encouraged to examine algebraic structures, or post-Pythagorean students could be challenged with a question such as: in a 45° isosceles triangle, what is the ratio of its sides?

Partitions and products

"I first came across this idea from an ATM publication: 'Points of Departure' . . . it is as good an idea for this century as it was for the last."

This task asks students to explore which partition of a given number produces the maximum product when re-written as a multiplication calculation.

Choose a number and ask each student to write four or five partitions. For example, using the number 10 one student might write:

5 + 5
2 + 3 + 5
4 + 5 + 1
1 + 1 + 1 + 1 + 1 + 1 + 1 + 1 + 1 + 1.

Now ask the student to change each addition sign into a multiplication sign and calculate the products:

5 x 5 = 25
2 x 3 x 5 = 30
4 x 5 x 1 = 20
1 x 1 x 1 x 1 x 1 x 1 x 1 x 1 x 1 x 1 = 1

Ask each student to provide one of their answers and write it on the board/screen, to let students see the different answers that are possible. A further task at this point can be for students to try to produce the partitions that led to the answers provided.

Binary monsters

"On one occasion a student drew a binary version of the Loch Ness monster."

These tasks are about coding and decoding: shifting between base 2 and base 10 numbers.

Here is a game to get students used to the idea of binary. Use the following binary monster grid:

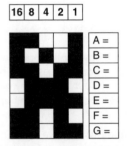

| 16 | 8 | 4 | 2 | 1 |

A =
B =
C =
D =
E =
F =
G =

Each horizontal row can now be coded by adding up the column headers for the squares that are filled in. So, if the first, second and fifth square are coloured for row A, then the row A total will be 16 + 8 + 1 = 25. A list of the totals for each row then becomes a code to describe a monster.

Once they have seen your example, students can then make their own monsters (without necessarily being restricted to the grid size shown) and work out the code for their monsters. This means converting base 2 to base 10 numbers.

Students can then swap codes with each other and use the code they have received to draw the same monster. Thus they are working from base 10 to base 2, thereby reversing the previous process.

Binary arithmetic

"Without the binary number system we would not have computers or mobile phones . . . in all it is a very powerful sequence."

This is another game which leads students gently into the fascinations of the binary system, eventually leading to 'bicimals' (a made-up word . . . but then aren't all words!), which are the base 2 equivalent of decimals in base 10.

Task 1: Give pairs of students the following set of numbers on pieces of card:

1	2	3	7	1

Tell them to see how far they can count by making combinations of these numbers, using addition only, without leaving any gaps. Using these numbers it is possible to get up to 25 with no gaps.

Task 2: As students achieve this outcome, give them five new pieces of paper and ask them to find five numbers that they can use to count from 1 up to more than 25. If no one achieves the highest total of 31, ask them to see if they can get even higher than the value they have currently achieved. If any pair shows they can count up to a total of 31 ask them to explain why they think this is the highest possible total?

Task 3: In teams of six allocate the numbers 16, 8, 4, 2, 1 on big pieces of card to five members of the team, sitting on chairs in a slight arc; the sixth member is to be the 'conductor'. Ask those who make a total of 19 to stand up.

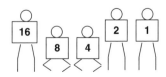

After a few further examples pose the task of forming all the counting numbers, in order, from 1 to 31; however, if anyone makes a mistake they are to start again at 1. The conductor has a major role to play in this task.

After 15 or so minutes to rehearse, ask groups to present their capability to produce all the numbers in order from 1 to 31; you could time these to see which group completes the task in the shortest amount of time. The main intention is for students to experience, first-hand how the binary system works, and this is further developed in the next idea.

Taking it further

Having generated these numbers students can develop their knowledge of the binary arithmetic system by generating all the values from 1 to 31 using the numbers 16, 8, 4, 2, 1 as column headings in a table. An important concept to recognise is that to generate numbers higher than 31 we need further columns with values of 32, 64 and so on. Patterns in the table can be observed and noted down (see the example at the end of this idea).

Base 2 or Binary column headings					
16	**8**	**4**	**2**	**1**	
				1	= 1
			1	0	= 2
			1	1	= 3
		1	0	0	= 4
		1	0	1	= 5
					= 6
					= 7
					= 8
					= 9
					= 10
					etc

Bicimals

"As students begin to understand the structure of bicimals they will deepen their knowledge of the place value system."

Bicimals are decimal fractions in base 2 and are equivalent to decimal fractions in base 10.

Teaching tip

Giving pairs of students a piece of rectangular paper and a pair of scissors to carry out the experiment reveals how rapidly each 'remaining' rectangle gets smaller and smaller.

This task considers how we can write fractions such as ⅓ in base 10 as bicimals in base 2. Students will need to be reminded of what the bicimals are as equivalent base 10 fractional values (½ = 0.1, ¼ = 0.01, ⅛ = 0.001 etc.).

To calculate ⅓ as a bicimal the following procedure might be helpful. Begin with a rectangle and cut it vertically and horizontally into four equal pieces. To share into three equal pieces you can give one piece to person A, one to B and one to C.

This leaves piece D, on which the process can be repeated, i.e. cut it into four equal sized pieces, E, F, G and H then share out three of them until you are left with an even smaller rectangular piece.

Taking it further

Having determined the bicimals equivalent for ⅓, what would ⅔ be? Explore fifths, starting with ⅕, then use this result to calculate bicimals for ⅖, ⅗, ⅘. Exploring tricimals as a bonus idea will stretch the most confident mathematicians, particularly seeking to write ¼ as a tricimal. You may wish to read an article from January 2013 in Mathematics Teaching (MT232) titled: *Perfect halving, bicimals and a toad-in-the-hole*.

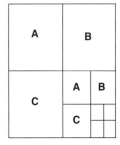

Discuss what happens next and what the different fractional amounts are in base 10 and what the equivalent bicimals values will be in base 2.

Fraction number line walls

"Having the different fractions displayed on the wall was helpful when we moved on to fraction arithmetic."

This is an alternative way of displaying fraction walls made from a series of strips of paper placed horizontally underneath each other to form fractional number lines.

Give the students some brightly coloured strips of paper and ask them to fold one into two equal length halves, another into three equal thirds, another into quarters, all the way down to twelfths. Students need to label their strips as illustrated in the online resource.

As students are puzzling out how to make the fractional amounts as accurately as possible there are rich opportunities for discussion about different methods students are using. For example, if they are given strips that are 21 cm long (or the approximate width of A4 paper) they might take a ruler to the situation.

By taking the strips of paper down to twelfths students can look for equivalent sets of fractions and compare fractional sizes, such as which is the biggest out of $\frac{2}{3}$ or $\frac{5}{7}$.

Sticking the completed sets of strips onto black sugar paper will make an attractive display that can be used for discussion and analysis.

Teaching tip

Students can work in pairs so they can help each other and discuss how they might make accurate folds. Some of the fraction folding will be easier and some will be connected, so once they have formed thirds, then sixths and twelfths will be not be too difficult. Fifths, sevenths and elevenths will require greater effort and concentration.

Taking it further

Ordering the fractions from smallest to largest (from $\frac{1}{12}$ to $\frac{11}{12}$) is a purposeful task as this helps reveal an interesting 'symmetry'.

Bonus idea ★

Make two strips for each fractional division and place one strip underneath the other. Write fractions on one strip and decimals on the other to let students see and compare the two types of notation. Make 'toblerone' shapes (or triangular-based prisms) with three rectangular faces. These can be used to write and compare fractions, decimals and percentages.

Fractions without fractiousness I

"Letting the students teach themselves how to add fractions worked much better than when I tried to teach them!"

This approach to adding and subtracting fractions is based upon folding A4 sheets of brightly coloured paper, where students can work out for themselves what either adding or subtracting fractions entails.

Teaching tip

When asking student to 'show' a third, two thirds, three thirds, a quarter, two quarters, three quarters and four quarters, simultaneously ask them to call out how many twelfths these form and record these on the board.

Taking it further

Having established $\frac{1}{3} + \frac{1}{4} = \frac{7}{12}$ (and not $\frac{2}{7}$) students can make up as many different questions as they can by adding a number of thirds and a number of quarters. When they are comfortable with addition, move on to subtraction.

Give everyone a sheet of A4 paper and ask students to fold into three equally wide strips, establishing that each strip is one third of the original piece of paper. Then ask them to fold the paper into four equal strips the other way, making a 3 by 4 grid.

Students should establish that each small piece is one twelfth of the whole piece of paper and write this on each of the 12 spaces.

By asking students to fold their pieces of paper into one third, two thirds, three thirds, one quarter, two quarters, three quarters and four quarters they can see for themselves what the equivalent amounts of twelfths are for each one and record each in their books. Establishing these equivalences is essential.

In pairs, ask one student to fold their paper into one quarter and the other student to fold theirs into one third, then to add their two fractions together. While some may not achieve the answer of $\frac{7}{12}$, either because they were not paying attention or they both folded the same fraction, the vast majority will achieve an answer of $\frac{7}{12}$.

Fractions without fractiousness II

"I want to see if students can decide for themselves the need to fold another piece of paper into thirds and fifths before I wade in with my size 10½s!"

This idea leads to students writing algebraic statements based upon systematically gathered data about adding (and subtracting) fractions.

Having established that students are comfortable with adding any amounts of thirds and quarters together, a next task is to ask them how they can add one third and one fifth together. By working in pairs they can discuss how to do this based upon how they added one third and one quarter together.

Some might be able to move directly to the use of equivalent fractions. Some might want to continue folding paper; they will clearly need to fold another (differently coloured) piece of paper into a 5 by 3 grid.

The intention is for students to again see 'what is going on' so they can begin to generalise that to add fractions with different denominators they need to find a fraction that is common to both: the common denominator.

Ask students to do several fraction additions where the numerator is always 1, for example, $\frac{1}{3} + \frac{1}{4} = \frac{7}{12}$, $\frac{1}{3} + \frac{1}{5} = \frac{8}{15}$, $\frac{1}{2} + \frac{1}{5} = \frac{7}{10}$, leading to them solving $1/p + 1/q$.

Teaching tip

Developing an expectation that students need to gather data in order to make sense of mathematics is an overriding pedagogic intention which you can choose to make explicit to those you teach.

Taking it further

Can students create an algebraic solution for $a/p + 1/q$? What about $a/p + b/q$?

IDEA 19

Fractions without fractiousness III

"When students determine mathematical 'rules' for themselves, their learning experience becomes more profound."

This idea focuses on students doing more paper folding in order to understand how to multiply and divide fractions and to develop the rules through generalising.

Teaching tip

For multiplying fractions students need to discuss what the word 'of' means mathematically. For division students need to discuss the different ways the word 'division' can be thought of. Ask students to make posters to describe how they multiply and divide fractions, using examples to illustrate their knowledge of these processes.

The concepts of multiplying and dividing fractions can be worked on using sheets of paper folded in the same way as in the previous ideas about fractions. Again students need lots of practice, gathering sufficient data, in order to see what is going on and to be encouraged to write algebraic formulae.

Multiplying fractions
Take a single sheet of folded paper (say thirds and fifths producing fifteenths). Having discussed what the word 'of' means, ask students to explore how to use their paper to work out what one third of two fifths is.

This can be done by first folding the paper into two fifths, then folding this into one third, to produce the following $2/15$ result.

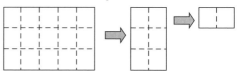

Checking that they arrive at the same answer by computing two fifths of one third, first folding the paper into one third then finding two fifths of that amount, is important.

Dividing fractions

Following discussion about how division is understood and defined, division of fractions requires students to work in groups of fours as follows.

If the calculation is $\frac{2}{5}$ divided by $\frac{1}{3}$ then one student can make two fifths, a second makes one third, another student provides the 'division arm' and the fourth can be the recorder.

With all these actors in place we just have to look at what $\frac{2}{5} \div \frac{1}{3}$ looks like:

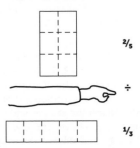

This clearly produces an answer of 6 (spaces) divided by 5 (spaces) or $\frac{6}{5}$.

This works because the fifteenths cancel out in the calculation:

$$\frac{\frac{6}{15}}{\frac{5}{15}}$$

This in fact is what occurs mathematically when we divide fractions: the common denominators of the two fractions cancel out.

Taking it further

Checking out the inverse calculation of $\frac{1}{3} \div \frac{2}{5}$, where the answer is $\frac{5}{6}$, will be useful. Ask students to explore what happens when the numerator is a whole number and the divisor is a fraction, for example, $3 \div \frac{1}{2}$ or $5 \div \frac{1}{4}$ etc. Challenge students to develop an algebraic formula for $a/p \div b/q$.

Fractions without fractiousness IV

"This rates as one of my top five ideas to use in the classroom!"

This idea begins by folding an isosceles right-angled triangle (IRAT) and can go as far as fractions with binary denominators having negative indices.

This idea begins as a demonstration, but by the end the students will be keen to try it for themselves. Make four IRATs from a square of paper by cutting along the diagonals. Take one, fold it down its line of symmetry, then cut along the fold line and ask the students to visualise what shapes you will have. There will be two half size IRATs, both similar to the original and congruent to each other; use this to lead into the meaning of similar and congruent.

Take a different coloured IRAT. Fold it down its line of symmetry then fold the shape a second time down its new line of symmetry. Cut along this second fold line, again asking students to visualise and make a sketch of what they think the resulting pieces will be. This time two IRATs with area $\frac{1}{4}$ and a square with area $\frac{1}{2}$ (of the original IRAT) are produced.

Three folds and a cut make four pieces: two triangles with area $\frac{1}{8}$, a triangle with area $\frac{1}{4}$ and a rectangle with area $\frac{1}{2}$. Ask students to write the fractional areas on each piece and check the fractions sum to 1, then let them loose with the paper and scissors!

What happens after four folds and a cut (down the final fold)? What about five folds and a cut? Each time students can check that each set of fractional pieces sums to 1.

As an extension for KS4 students, begin by identifying IRATs of the following fractional sizes:

- $\frac{1}{2}$ from one fold and a cut
- $\frac{1}{4}$ from two folds and a cut
- $\frac{1}{8}$ from three folds and a cut
- $\frac{1}{16}$ from four folds and a cut
- $\frac{1}{32}$ from five folds and a cut.

Ascertain that $\frac{1}{2}$ can be written as $\frac{1}{2}^1$, $\frac{1}{4}$ as $\frac{1}{2}^2$ etc. Working upwards from the IRAT size gained from five folds we have the following pattern:

IRAT as a fraction in index form	Area
$\frac{1}{2}^5$	$\frac{1}{32}$
$\frac{1}{2}^4$	$\frac{1}{16}$
$\frac{1}{2}^3$	$\frac{1}{8}$
$\frac{1}{2}^2$	$\frac{1}{4}$
$\frac{1}{2}^1$	$\frac{1}{2}$

By continuing the rows, the next two lines will be:

$\frac{1}{2}^0$	1
$\frac{1}{2}^{-1}$	2

This provides students with a triangular piece of paper whose area is written as a fraction with a negative index.

Taking it further

For four folds and a cut students should have six pieces. Can they rearrange them back to make the original IRAT? What about for five folds, when there will be nine pieces?

25

Playing with percentages

"Using a 'flipped classroom' approach, where students find out about percentages and how to increase and decrease by percentage amounts can create more powerful learning than with a traditional teaching approach."

Finding problems for students to solve, where they can change and control variables and look for patterns and seek connections, can be a useful way of making percentages more palatable.

One way to increase an amount of money by a certain percentage is to carry out a two stage calculation as follows:

1 Calculate the increase.
2 Add this increase onto the initial amount.

For example if you start with £34 and increase this by 10%, you calculate 10% of £34 (which is £3.40) then add £3.40 onto £34 making a total of £37.40. This is the long route.

A short route is to carry out a single multiplication calculation only. In other words, find out what you need to multiply 34 by to gain the answer 37.4?

Ask students to play around with some multiplication calculations to try to achieve this.

Tell them that when they think they have worked out what the multiplier or the scale factor is, they should check their ideas by working out some more long cuts and short cuts beginning with different amounts:

- What will the short cut for a 20% increase or a 5% increase?
- What about a 10% decrease or 20% and 5% decreases?

Rooting out square roots I

"Being able to estimate square roots of numbers is a valuable skill in many contexts, for example when determining whether a number is prime or not."

This idea is for students to develop the concept of a square root beginning with some work on squaring and finding areas of squares.

Ask students to calculate the following products: $1 \times 1, 2 \times 2, 3 \times 3, 4 \times 4 \ldots 10 \times 10$. Having gained the square numbers from 1 to 100, the next step is to calculate the following products: $1.5 \times 1.5, 2.5 \times 2.5, 3.5 \times 3.5, 9.5 \times 9.5$, perhaps utilising the grid method:

Teaching tip

By drawing diagrams on 1 cm squared paper to represent calculations such as 3.5×3.5, students can check for themselves (by counting squares) the reasonableness of their calculations. Indeed, for students to recognise that 3.5×3.5 is the same as $(3.5)^2$ which, in turn, is the same as the area of a square of side length $3\frac{1}{2}$ is an important connection to make.

x	3	0.5
3	9	1.5
0.5	1.5	0.25

By this stage students will have a list of 19 calculations together with their squares (numerically and pictorially). These can now be graphed, labelling the x-axis as the length of the side of a square and the y-axis as the area of a square.

Once the graph has been drawn students can use it to determine the approximate areas of squares with side lengths such as 3.8, 5.3 and so on, and then check, with or without their calculators, the accuracy of their 'by eye' estimates.

Rooting out square roots II

"So many skills and concepts can be drawn together when studying square roots such as: area, surds, irrational numbers, rounding, graphs . . ."

This idea gives students first-hand experience of calculating square roots by approximation and multiplication and, in doing so, gives them a deep understanding of the concept of a square root.

Teaching tip

By working in pairs students can discuss how close their approximations are, to two decimal places, to the required answers.

Taking it further

Use the same approximation method, with a calculator, to determine the cube roots of numbers or to find the length of a cube given its volume.

Ask students to consider how they can use the graph drawn earlier in idea 22 to find the length of the side of a square with area 75 (square units). This should produce answers of either 8.6 or 8.7.

By examining the resulting products, 73.96 and 75.69, students can explore how close to 75 they can get by squaring a value to two decimal places.

Ask students to choose their own values (which are not perfect squares) such as 28 or 60 and use the processes of reading from the graph and using their calculators to gain more accurate answers to two decimal places.

Bonus idea ★

Students could also use the process of square rooting to determine whether a number is prime or not. For example to determine whether 137 is prime, students need to gain an estimate of the square root of 137, which is greater than 12 and less than 13. They then only need to consider whether the prime numbers, less than 12 are a factor of 137. This, in turn builds upon students' capabilities to carry out divisibility tests.

Playing with data

"A great way to get students using and applying mathematical skills and concepts."

This idea involves students being given certain conditions or parameters. They then have to create data sets which meet them.

Ask students to write a data set where the mode is 7. It will be interesting to see if anyone writes a data set with just one piece of information, i.e. the number 7. The purpose of this opening question is to show that without certain conditions there will be an infinite number of solutions.

The next step is to add some parameters: create a data set with four whole number values less than 10, where the mode is 7.

Again there will be many different answers so we can suggest another parameter: create a data set with four values less than 10 and a range of 5 where the mode is 7.

Further questions can be posed:

- Create a data set with values less than 10, where the mode is 7 and the median is 6.
- Create a data set, using positive values only, which has a mode of 4, a median of 5 and a mean of 6.
- What would the minimum range be for such a data set?

Teaching tip

The ideas intentionally start with very easy questions which have open-ended answers. This can lead to interesting discussions about the importance of parameters.

Bonus idea

Each of the ideas in the main idea would be suitable for KS3 students; the following would be more challenging questions for KS4 or even KS5 students:

- If we had the data 14, 34, 36, 56, 59, 68, explain how each of the range, mean, median and standard deviation would change if the 14 were changed to 10.
- If we had the data 14, 34, 36, 56, 59, 68, explain how each of the range, mean, median and standard deviation would change if the 34 were changed to 64?

Unjamming the log jam

"I find it no surprise how many students find logarithms something of a mystery as they are something of a complex concept."

This idea involves students creating a $\log_{10}$ table from first principles in order to get underneath what logarithms are and how they can be constructed. Before beginning this idea it is important for students to revisit the laws of indices where:
$n^p \times n^q = n^{(p+q)}$ **and** $n^p \div n^q = n^{(p-q)}$

Students need to explore what happens when we square root the square root of 10, square root the cube root of 10, cube root the square root of 10, square the cube root of 10, cube root the cube root of 10 etc. For example, the square root of the square root of 10 will be approximately 1.78, which is the same as $10^{1/4}$.

A good starting point for this idea is revising calculations involving indices such as:

$2^3 \times 2^5 = 8 \times 32$ $3^2 \times 3^4 = 9 \times 81$ $5^6 \div 5^4 = 15625 \div 625$
$8 \times 32 = 256$ $9 \times 81 = 729$ $15625 \div 625 = 25$
$256 = 2^8$ $729 = 3^6$ $25 = 5^2$

Students will also need to be comfortable with concepts such as: $\sqrt{a} = a^{1/2}$ and the cube root of a value 'a' is $\sqrt[3]{a} = a^{1/3}$

Ask students to use their calculators to check out two results to two places of decimal:

$10^{1/2} = 3.16$
$10^{1/3} = 2.15$

The intention now is to use fractional indices to gather further information to determine the value of expressions such as $10^{(1/2 + 1/3)}$. Ideally you want students to think about how they can do this in order to understand $10^{5/6} = 6.79$ (or 3.16×2.15).

Students can use the information they gain to gather more data, for example:

Power of 10 as a fraction	Power of 10 in decimal notation	Result to two decimal places
$\frac{1}{2}$	0.5	3.16
$\frac{1}{3}$	0.33	2.15
$\frac{1}{4}$	0.25	1.78
$\frac{5}{6}$	0.833	6.81
$\frac{1}{6}$	0.166	1.47
...		
...		

Tell students to use this information to estimate other fractional powers of $10^{x/y}$ then to use their calculators to see how close they were.

Taking it further

The second and third columns can now be turned into co-ordinate pairs and graphed.

Again, assuming students at this level will be comfortable with the idea $10^0 = 1$, the graph of $\log_{10}$ can be drawn in the first quadrant.

Discuss the connection between the two equations:

i) $10^a = b$

ii) $\log_{10}b = a$.

Choose three numbers

"I always look for opportunities for students to pose and solve each other's mathematical problems; in this way they gain greater ownership of the work they do."

This sequence of tasks is aimed at manipulating numbers using addition, subtraction, multiplication, co-ordinates, area and perimeter calculations . . . all with just three numbers.

Ask the students to choose three positive whole numbers, each less than 10, and use them to complete the following tasks.

- Addition task: Add them in pairs to produce three totals, so choosing 5, 6 and 9 will give totals of 11, 14 and 15. Give the totals to a partner to double check the calculations.
- Multiplication task: As above but this time calculate the three products, giving 30, 45 and 54.
- Multiplication and addition task: This time multiply two numbers and add the third, producing answers of 39, 51 and 59.
- Multiplication and subtraction task: Multiply two numbers and subtract the third, producing 21, 39 and 49.
- Co-ordinate task A: Create three pairs of co-ordinates based upon arithmetic order, for example, (5, 6), (5, 9) and (6, 9). Plot the points and see what happens. Calculate the area of the shape formed.
- Co-ordinate task B: This time plot the points in reverse arithmetic order, for example, (6, 5), (9, 5) and (9, 6). In what way is the second shape related to the first?
- Co-ordinate task C: This time plot all six points to form a hexagon and calculate its area.

Number, algebra and proof

Part 2

The joy of algebra I

"Algebra should be a joy . . . but as we know it is frequently seen as a pointless waste of time . . . why is this?"

These ideas provide students with opportunities to use and apply algebra; the algebra arises from problem-solving contexts based upon numerical calculations.

Depending upon the class, you might want to start with a discussion about what a 2-digit number actually means, for example, $72 = 7 \times 10 + 2 \times 1$, $35 = 3 \times 10 + 5 \times 1$, leading to ab (when representing a 2-digit number) is equal to $a \times 10 + b \times 1$ or $10a + b$.

Ask students to write a two digit number using two different digits, for example, 72. Ask them to reverse the number and find the difference, for example, $72 - 27 = 45$. Collect a boardful of examples then ask students to work in pairs or a group of three to discuss the results and see if they can work out what the answer is going to be, just by looking at the two digits originally chosen.

The next step is to ask students, again working in a pair or a group of three, to write what the 'answer' would be if the two digits were a and b.

What happens with a 3-digit number? What about 4- or 5-digit numbers?

The joy of algebra II

"Algebra helps us make sense of why something works the way it does."

This idea provides students with a further opportunity to use and apply algebra. As in the previous task students need to be confident about writing a general 2-digit number *ab* in the form 10a + b.

Ask students to write three different digits, for example, 7, 1, 4. Now use these to make all possible 2-digit numbers, for example, 71, 14, 74, 17, 41, 47. Next find the sum of these six 2-digit numbers: 264. Divide this total by 22 and write the answer: 12.

Now return to the original three single digits and add them together: 7 + 1 + 4 = 12 (again). Providing students have followed the procedure correctly they will find the answer to the total of the sum of the six 2-digit numbers when divided by 22 is equal to the sum of the three original digits. The question is why?

Encourage students to use algebra to try to explain why this happens.

Try starting with four single digits; what do you need to divide by in order for the puzzle to work? What about five single digits? What about starting with any amount (*n*) of single digits? Can students determine what the dividing factor must be for the puzzle to work?

Teaching tip

Asking students to write about what happens and to explain why it happens is a powerful way of helping them become explicit about their learning.

Taking it further

What happens if you start with three digits and find all possible 3-digit numbers? What will the dividing factor be now? What about choosing all 3-digit numbers from four digits?

Fibonacci I

"The Fibonacci sequence is yet another fascinating feature of mathematics."

These ideas consider four ways to generate the Fibonacci sequence, together with some ways the sequence can be explored and analysed.

Students can explore the sequence and see what patterns and connections they can find. For example, can they explain why the sequence runs odd, odd, even, odd, odd, even?

Generating Fibonacci 1: Going up steps. Assuming that you ascend steps either one at a time or two at a time, how many different step patterns will there be for different numbers of steps? With five steps there are eight patterns: 1,1,1,1,1; 1,1,1,2; 1,1,2,1; 1,2,1,1; 2,1,1,1; 1,2,2; 2,1,2; 2,2,1.

Generating Fibonacci 2: How many ways can you put either £1 or £2 coins into a parking meter to pay a £5 parking fee? Again the same eight patterns will be possible.

Generating Fibonacci 3: With five large paving slabs measuring 1 m by 2 m, how many ways can a 5 m path be laid? For example:

Again there will be eight different paths.

How many different ways will there be of ascending steps, putting coins into a meter or laying a path for different amount of steps, parking fees or paths?

Choose any three consecutive terms, square the middle term and find the product of the outside terms . . . what happens? Explore the Lucas sequence, which follows the same pattern as the Fibonacci sequence but starts with the numbers 2 and 1. Compare these with the Fibonacci sequence.

Generating Fibonacci 4: Using a spreadsheet type '1' in cell A1, '1' in cell A2, '= A1 + A2' in cell A3 then drag the cursor down from cell A3 and fill down (Ctrl D).

Fibonacci II

"So much more to explore . . . so little time."

These ideas lend themselves to deeper algebraic thinking.

Task 1: Ask students to create some sequences with five terms following the Fibonacci pattern, for example, 5, 6, 11, 17, 28 or 6, 1, 5, 4, 9 and challenge them to find a connection between the middle term and the first and last terms. Can they write this connection algebraically? What if the sequences have seven or nine terms?

Task 2: Ask students to write any pair of positive whole numbers and perform a Fibonacci type routine to generate ten terms, for example, 7, 3, 10, 13, 23, 36, 59, 95, 154, 249. If they sum the sequence, they should get the same number as if they multiply the seventh term in the sequence by 11: 59 x 11 = 7 + 3 + 10 + 13 + 23 + 36 + 59 + 95 + 154 + 249 = 649.

Try this for any pair of starting numbers, extending to negative, fractional or decimal values. Can students explain why the seventh term when multiplied by 11 is equal to the sum of the ten terms?

Taking it further

Create sequences, either using pencil and paper or on a spreadsheet, based upon Fibonacci type sequences whose first two numbers are: a) 1, 2 b) 1, 3 c) 1, 4 and so on. Now compare the sequences of numbers, for example the fourth terms will be 5, 7 and 9 and the fifth terms will be 8, 11, 14. Ask students to find the nth terms for these sequences.

Fibonacci III

"At the supermarket checkout the other day I noticed a young woman whose name badge read 'Phi'. I asked her if she knew what the phi meant and when I told her it was something to do with the golden ratio she quickly replied 'Does that make me a "Golden girl"?'"

Another way to explore the beauty of the Fibonacci sequence.

Ask students to write the Fibonacci sequence twice, with the first starting at 1, 2 and the second starting at 1, 1. They should generate about 20 terms for each one. Line these sequences up as shown in the table.

Sequence A starting 1, 2	Sequence B starting 1,1	Dividing A by B	Creating co-ordinate pairs
1	1	1	(1, 1)
2	1	2	(2, 2)
3	2	1.5	(3, 1.5)
5	3	1.6 (recurring)	(4, 1.667)
8	5	1.625	(5, 1.6)
...	...	...	...

As students approach the twentieth term divided by the twentieth term what do they notice? This value has a special name, the Golden Ratio, and is denoted by the Greek symbol ϕ (phi).

What happens if the calculation is reversed, so that values in sequence B are divided by values in sequence A?

Suggest students draw a graph by generating co-ordinate pairs (1, 1), (2, 2), (3, 1.5), (4, 1.666), (5, 1.6) etc. On the same pair of axes they should draw a graph to illustrate what happens with the reverse calculation. What do they notice?

Taking it further

Setting up and solving the quadratic equation $\phi^2 - \phi = 1$ arising from $1/\phi = \phi - 1$.

Thus the twentieth term divided by the nineteenth term (starting from 1, 1, 2, 3, 5 etc) is $6765 \div 4181 = 1.618034$ (to six decimal places) and the inverse is $4181 \div 6765$ which is 0.618034, so the inverse is 1 less than the original calculation. Expressing this as a generality we have $1/\phi = \phi - 1$ which is $\phi^2 - \phi = 1$ or $\phi^2 - \phi - 1 = 0$.

Bonus idea ★

An interesting project is to ask students to research how the Fibonacci numbers and the Golden Ratio appear in natural forms. This could even be an opportunity to take mathematics outside the classroom!

Square numbers

"I was surprised one day when teaching a new Year 9 class to find the students had not met the notion of a square number being represented as a square area."

There are three obvious ways to generate square numbers. These ideas encourage exploration of squares.

Pose the following questions to your students:

- Why can't a square number have a unit digit of 2?
- What other unit digits can square numbers have and not have?

The classic problem of how many squares on a chessboard leads to the summation of square numbers. For example in a 3 by 3 square there are 14 squares: nine 1 by 1, four 2 by 2 and one 3 by 3. This can be represented as $3^2 + 2^2 + 1^2$.

You can set a similar puzzle looking at the number of triangles in different sized equilateral triangles drawn on isometric grid paper.

Teaching tip

Start by letting students tell you everything they already know about square numbers in order to set the scene for future exploration.

Taking it further

Explore which numbers between 1 and 100 are the sum of two square numbers. This task could provide some pre-Pythagoras type work.

Bonus idea ★

Observe and discuss with the students how square numbers can be made from consecutive triangle numbers:

$1 + 3 = 4$

$3 + 6 = 9$

$6 + 10 = 16$ and so on.

Other patterns can be made by adding and subtracting square numbers, or by summing consecutive cube numbers. What do the students notice about these patterns?

Five numbers in a ring

". . . knowledge does not fall neatly into separate compartments and that work and play are not opposites but complementary." (Plowden repot, 1967, para 505)

Playing with numbers through all kinds of puzzles is an important way of developing number confidence.

Ask students to write the numbers 1, 2, 3, 4 and 5 in any order in a (pentagonal) ring, calculate the positive difference between adjacent pairs of numbers, and write the answers in between each pair (perhaps in another colour to differentiate them from the five starting numbers). Then sum these differences, writing the total in the middle of the ring.

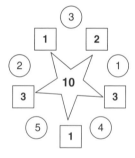

What other totals can be achieved using the same five starting numbers written in a different order? Discuss how the totals have been created. How can students be sure there are no other totals to be found? What happens if you start with six, seven or eight consecutive numbers? How many different totals are there for each situation?

Having explored the sum, try the same exercise but calculate the product or quotient of each pair instead. For the quotient you will need to determine a direction of travel around the ring, and try the exercise in each direction.

Going dotty

"There are two reasons why arithmetic . . . always make a strong appeal to children . . . They like it for the same reason they like puzzles and riddles. It gives them pleasurable mental activity without strain." (*Modern teaching in the infant school*, 1931, p139)

This is a simple, accessible idea that has layers of potential complexities. All students need to be able to do is to make some dots and join them together with straight lines.

The problem is to see how many 'different' arrangements of a given number of dots are possible, and how many joins exist for these arrangements. This connects ideas of geometric arrangements with simple counting and some algebraic generalisation, and as such it would be suitable for students from a wide age range.

Teaching tip

Try to leave the problem open, so that students can engage with some ambiguity and make their own decisions about how to arrange the dots and how many joins are possible.

Set up this idea by asking a number of students to draw five dots on the board/screen, and join them with straight lines. Having collected some examples, ask the students to analyse them.

One student might draw five dots in a straight line, with four joins. If one of the dots is placed above the other four then there are seven joins:

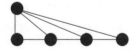

The joins must be straight lines, but need not be the same length. They can cross over each other.

How many different arrangements/number of joins are possible? Ask students to:

- classify the types of structures created
- search for number patterns.

Can students generalise the sets of results formed for different numbers of dots and types of arrangements?

Taking it further

Explore 'impossible cases'. For example, with four dots it is impossible to have exactly four join lines. What are the impossible cases for other numbers of dots?

4-square meeting point problem

"A problem once described as a GCSE coursework task but a cracking good idea to integrate into any scheme of work!"

This problem involves students collecting data, analysing it and seeking to form algebraic generalisations. The task is to explore connections between the number of squares, the perimeter and the number of 4-square meeting points.

Teaching tip

This idea can be used with Year 10 students in mixed-attainment groups. Because the problem can be both simplified and developed to varying degrees, all students can experience achievement.

The diagram below is made from 12 squares. The marked points show places where four squares meet. The perimeter of this shape is 20.

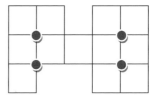

We now have three pieces of data:

- number of squares = 12
- perimeter = 20
- number of 4-square meeting points = 3.

Ask students to create different arrangements of 12 squares, and find the perimeter and number of 4-square meeting points for each arrangement. What patterns can they find? What happens if they start with a different number of squares?

Extend the idea by exploring 3-square, 2-square and 1-square meeting points.

Bonus idea ★

A similar problem can be set using equilateral triangles. Do the same patterns emerge?

$x + y = 10$

"Tasks that connect together different ideas and concepts help students make greater sense of mathematics."

This idea is one way to introduce students to equations of straight lines from the simple starting point of asking them to provide two positive whole numbers which add up to 10.

Ask volunteers to come to the board/screen and each write a pair of positive whole numbers that add up to ten. Once a collection of possible answers have been generated, ask students to:

- write the results in an ordered way
- turn the pairs of values into co-ordinate pairs
- plot the results as a graph.

Once the line (of $x + y = 10$) has been drawn, further questions can be asked.

- What if one of the values is 4½?
- Does 'this' point i.e. (4½, 5½) also sit on the line?
- What if one of the values is 3.8?
- Where does this point lie on the graph?
- How many different answers are possible now?
- What happens if one of the two numbers is 13?

These questions are aimed at moving away from positive integer values by extending the range to fractions, decimals and negative values. There is also the notion of infinity lurking around.

Repeat the exercise with pairs of numbers that add up to 8. What do the students notice? How do the two graphs compare?

Teaching tip

Deciding when it is appropriate to ask students what the 'name' of the graph is could be a critical point in the first lesson.

Taking it further

Extend the problem to further pairs of numbers:

- one number subtract another equals 5
- one number subtract another equals minus 5
- double one number and add another to make 10.

100 square

"Unlocking students' understanding of linear sequences lays foundations for advanced level mathematics."

This idea develops the concept that any linear sequence can be determined by knowing the base set of multiples upon which a sequence is formed.

Create an extended 100 square by having a 14 by 14 grid with the normal 100 square in the centre. Extend the bottom line so that it covers −1 to 12, and extend some of the other lines in the same way; this means that some numbers will be repeated on the grid. Each student will need a completed copy of the extended grid and a piece of tracing paper.

Ask students to place the tracing paper over the grid and draw separate circles on the tracing paper to cover the first four or five multiples of 2, i.e. 2, 4, 6, 8, 10. Then walk them through the following procedure.

- Establish that the circled values can be described as $2n$ numbers.
- Shift the tracing paper one place to the left, so the numbers 1, 3, 5, 7, 9 become circled.
- Establish that a shift of one place to the left is the same as −1. This new sequence of numbers can, therefore, be described algebraically as $2n - 1$.

Returning each time to the circled numbers 2, 4, 6, 8, 10, different shifts can be made, for example, two places to the left to create the sequence $2n - 2$, three places to the right creates $2n + 3$, one place up creates $2n + 10$.

The crux aspect of the task now follows. Students should circle the first four or five numbers in a set of multiples. If they choose the multiples of 7 then, on their tracing paper, they will circle the values covering 7, 14, 21, 28 and 35. Having done this they choose a shift; suppose this is one row up and two spaces to the left. This means that the new circled numbers will be 15, 22, 29, 36 and 43. The student knows (is intended to know!) that they have made a shift of +8 (+10 − 2) for each of the values in their base sequence (multiples of 7), so the algebraic description for the new values must be $7n + 8$.

Supply students with strips of sugar paper measuring approximately 10 cm by 30 cm and felt pens. Ask them to write down their sequences, but not the algebraic description, and display them around the room. In no time at all many linear sequences will emerge. The next step is for students to work out the algebraic description of each displayed sequence. This gives them an opportunity to practise how to write nth terms from existing sequences, having already created their own.

Rectangling

"Students often mix up concepts of area and perimeter and I wonder if this is partly due to insufficient energy being focused on the difference between length as a 1D measure and area as a 2D measure."

This idea is about exploring rectangles in terms of their dimensions and how these determine perimeters and areas.

Ask students to draw half a dozen or so rectangles on 1 cm squared paper. Using these rectangles ask them to fill in a table with the headings:

- Dimensions in cm[1] (for example, 3 by 5)
- Perimeter (P) in cm[1] (for example, 16)
- Area (A) in cm[2] (for example, 15)
- Comparing P with A (for example, P > A).

Can the students find conditions and construct rules by which P > A and P < A?

The following explanation should not be given verbatim to students, but may be used to nudge them in an interesting direction!

Consider rectangles with a fixed dimension of 5 and a varying dimension of n, where n is any number. The perimeter of this set of rectangles will be $5 + 5 + n + n$ (or $10 + 2n$), and the area will be $5 \times n$ (or $5n$).

To determine where the perimeter and the area are equal, you can use the equation $10 + 2n = 5n$. Solving this gives $n = 3\frac{1}{3}$.

Returning to integer values, any 5-by rectangle with the other dimension 3 or less will fall into the category P > A, and any 5-by rectangle where the other dimension is 4 or greater, will fall into the P < A category.

Diagonal diversions

"Using problems which require students to use and apply both Pythagoras' theorem and trigonometry are far more powerful for students' understanding than ploughing through meaningless exercises from a textbook."

The following problems are based upon lengths of lines and areas of shapes within regular polygons. The problems are written for students who have acquired knowledge of Pythagoras and trigonometry.

In a regular pentagon all diagonals are the same length. What is the ratio of the length of a diagonal to the length of a side in a regular pentagon?

Teaching tip

Students who engage with mathematics at this level of sophistication would be expected to ascribe a unit measure (of length 1) to the edge length of the shapes they work with.

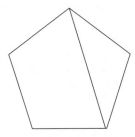

The result of comparing the edge length to diagonal length of the regular pentagon is 1.618 (to three decimal places), i.e. the Golden Ratio (ϕ). This task can be used to create the quadratic $\phi^2 - \phi - 1 = 0$, arising from $1/\phi = \phi - 1$.

As in the diagram above, a regular pentagon is partitioned into two areas with a single diagonal slice; an isosceles triangle and an isosceles trapezium are formed. What is the ratio of the areas of these shapes?

Taking it further

A regular hexagon has two diagonals of different lengths. Explore how the lengths of these diagonals compare with the edge length of the hexagon. How do the areas of different possible shapes compare?

Card trickery

"A former headteacher showed me this trick and I have used it many times since."

This idea is about unravelling the mathematics behind a card trick, with an opportunity for students to create an algebraic formula.

Demonstrate the trick first. Using a full pack of cards, turn over the first one and call out its face value (J, Q, K count as face value of 10). Count out the extra cards required so that the face value of the first card and the number of extra cards add to 12. For example, if the first card is a 9 then count three more cards to make 12. Place these three cards face down on top of the 9 (which will be face up). This makes the first pile (p).

Turn over the next card from the remaining pack and repeat as before. If this card is a 5 then count out a further seven cards (to make up to 12); place these face down on top of the 5, to make a second pile.

Keep repeating this until you reach a situation where there are not enough cards in the remaining pack to add to 12. Place these cards in a separate remainder pile (r). Now turn over each pile, so the top cards are face down.

It is possible to work out the total (T) of the face-down cards by knowing how many piles (p) and how many remainder cards (r) there are.

Now challenge the students to work out why the trick works.

More rectangling

"Mathematics is essentially about looking for patterns, seeking connections and trying to make sense of them."

This idea develops students' understanding of quadratic sequences. It requires students to have access to 1 cm square grid paper.

Ask the students to draw a rectangle on square grid paper, for example 7 by 4. They should then choose a grid point on one edge of the rectangle, but not at a corner, and draw horizontal and vertical lines, which do not meet or cross each other, to create a path to the opposite side (again not to a corner) as in the example below.

Teaching tip

Students can fix one side first, and generalise the other, for example, 7 by n. What happens with 6 by n rectangles?

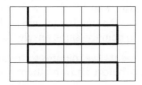

The path above is constructed of 4×1 vertical and 3×5 horizontal components, making a total of 19. The challenge is to find the longest possible path between parallel sides.

Traversing the other pair of parallel edges gives the following longest-path diagram.

Taking it further

Construct formulae for the longest path for the general m by n rectangle.

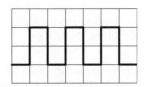

Here there are 6×2 vertical and 7×1 horizontal components, again making a total of 19.

Ask students to choose other pairs of dimensions and see what the different paths and their components are.

Bonus idea ★

What happens if the problem is based upon an equilateral triangle drawn on an isometric-dot grid? For this problem the idea is to move from a point on one side (similarly not at a corner) to either of the other two sides, again taking the longest route possible. Perhaps unsurprisingly, the result is connected to, though not the same as, the triangular number sequence.

Number route problems

"Because it (setting) is not allowed in Taiwan. If it was, less advanced students would feel they are being labelled. It's like saying they'll never advance; their class mates would treat them differently. So this (mixed attainment) policy respects the children's psychological development." (Hau, Lee, L. *Worlds Apart*, BBC Panorama 3 June 1996)

The phrase 'students being responsible for their learning' is one that springs to mind with an idea such as 'number route problems'. Here students set up and solve each other's problems, thus creating a culture of problem posing and solving.

Teaching tip

Modelling this process, so students know what they need to do to create their own number routes, is an important aspect for them to develop underlying skills and concepts.

Taking it further

Suggest students choose starting values for *n* which are fractional, decimal and/or negative. They can play with the basic structure by performing a division calculation somewhere in the process, or subtracting an amount.

Demonstrate the process with an example first. Tell the students that you have:

- chosen a number (*n*) and multiplied it by 6 to gain an answer (*a*)
- added 24 to the number (*n*) and multiplied this by 2 to gain the same answer (*a*).

Give the students five minutes to try to find your *n* and *a*, before showing them how to do it algebraically.

Clearly trial and improvement can be used to provide the correct values for *n* and *a*. However, this task also has rich potential for students to practise and consolidate solving equations with an unknown on both sides.

The example above can be represented as the two equations $6n = a$ and $(n + 24) \times 2 = a$. These can be combined to form the equality $6n = 2n + 48$. Solving this gives $n = 12$ and $a = 72$.

Now tell students to pair up and set their own problems for each other. They can use a similar structure, but change the multiplying factors and the amount they add.

Multiplying mayhem

"Causing students to explore multiplication through a variety of problems is a valuable way of helping them become more confident multipliers."

This problem is an exploration of the traditional multiplication system on a square grid turned through 45°.

Introduce the symbol 'ʂ' as the multiplication symbol when using a square grid turned through 45°. On the turned grid, draw a three-dot by two-dot array. Counting the number of dots in the array gives a total of 8.

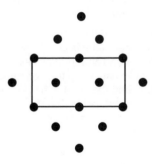

Tell the students that in this system, therefore, 3 ʂ 2 = 8. Can they work out 5 ʂ 3? What about 7 ʂ 2?

As students get to grips with the new system, give them some more challenging questions.

- What are the square numbers in this system?
- What is the general term for a square number n ʂ n?
- What is the general term for a rectangular number m ʂ n?
- What are the prime numbers in this system?

Algebra through paper folding

"Algebra is only ever any use for the purposes of solving problems and describing structures within mathematics."

This is another opportunity for students to use and apply algebra within a problem-solving context. The tasks are based upon creating simple rectangles by paper folding and ascribing variables to the dimensions in order to prove why certain results occur.

Provide each student with three pieces of A6 paper and ask them to write the dimensions l and w on one of them.

Having ascertained the area of the rectangle is lw and the perimeter is $2l + 2w$ ask students to take the second and third pieces of paper and fold one in half along the horizontal line of symmetry and the other in half along the vertical line of symmetry. Can the students work out the areas and the perimeters of the new shapes?

How can they prove that one of the new shapes has a greater perimeter than the other? Challenge students to find all the different possible perimeters of compound shapes formed from the two new rectangles. For example:

If students are allowed to overlap shapes, how many different perimeters can be made?

Proof of the pudding

"Proof is the ultimate process, the pinnacle of mathematical thinking."

This is a selection of problems, all based upon developing students' capability to use algebra in order to prove statements.

- Draw a 2 by 2 square around any four numbers in a 99 square. Prove that when you add the two largest values and subtract the two smallest values, the answer will always be 20.
- Draw a 2 by 2 square around any four numbers in a 99 square. Prove that when you multiply pairs of diagonal values together the difference is 10. What happens if you start with a 3 by 3 square?
- Prove why the addition of any two odd numbers is equal to an even number.
- Prove that the product of any two odd numbers is always odd.
- Prove that the difference between the squares of any two consecutive numbers is equal to their sum.
- Prove that the difference between any consecutive pair of square numbers is always an odd number.

Teaching tip

For students to become confident with algebraic manipulation they need to be fluent with ideas such as:

- two consecutive numbers can be written algebraically as n and $(n + 1)$
- any odd number can be written algebraically as $(2n - 1)$
- a pair of consecutive odd numbers is $(2n - 1)$ and $(2n + 1)$
- the square of an odd number is $(2n - 1)^2$ which expands to $4n^2 - 4n + 1$.

2D Geometry problems

Part 3

Battle-blobs

"Logic is a fundamental aspect of mathematics, underpinning systems and structures, meanings and conventions."

This is a logic game for two players. It is similar to 'Battleships', but far more complicated, involving deeper strategic thinking.

Player A draws an 8 by 8 grid and secretly places an agreed number of blobs inside the grid.

Player B then selects places at the edge of the grid, using a co-ordinate-type system, from which to send rays into the grid. Player A must determine the path of each ray, and tell player B where it will exit the grid. Player B attempts to find the positions of the blobs using the lowest possible number of rays.

A ray cannot move past a blob that is either in a direct line or on a line immediately next to a blob.

- If a ray hits a blob 'full on' then it is absorbed. So in the diagram on the next page, a ray entering at **F8** is absorbed and player A says: 'Absorbed'.
- When a ray meets a blob on an adjacent line, the ray is deflected at right angles and continues following this new path until it either exits or meets another blob. A ray entering at **A4** exits the grid at **A1**.
- If a ray meets a single space between two blobs, it is reflected back the way it came. A ray entering at **E1** will be reflected back and exit at **E1**.
- A ray entering at **H4** takes a double deflection and exits at **H3**.
- Similarly to the above, a ray entering at **E8** exits at **E6**.
- Rays entering at either **D8** or **D1** will both be absorbed (by the blob in space **D2**)

The winner of each game is the person who took the smallest number of goes (or used the smallest number of rays) in order to find their partner's four blobs.

See what happens when a ray enters at **A3** – this is a very interesting route to follow. If you have understood the rules you should find it exits at the same place, **A3**, after seven 'encounters' and eight movements on the grid.

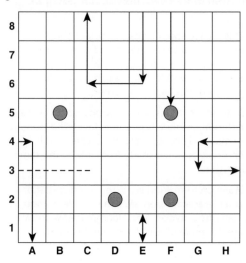

Taking it further

This idea uses a 'closed' set of processes but is an open task as there are many different places four blobs can be placed. Four blobs is the usual amount but more blobs will lead to a more complicated game. The game could also be played as a whole class knock-out competition, or could be given to a class as an interesting puzzle, challenging them to determine how many first round byes there would need to be so that, after the first round the number of contestants reduce as follows: 32, 61, 8, 4, 2, 1 (the winner).

Fun with tessellations

"Tessellations are a valuable aspect of the interface between art and mathematics; creativity abounds."

Tessellations are formed using regular polygons. Semi-regular tessellations are formed from more than one regular polygon.

This idea is about creating regular and semi-regular tessellations and examining the angles of the polygons used. The rule for any tessellation is that the same number of polygons meet at each corner.

Provide lots of regular polygons, using as many different colours as possible. Invite the students to make regular tessellations, where each different design is made from lots of the same polygon.

Move on to making semi-regular tessellations, where each different design is made of more than one polygon. The diagram below shows one example of a semi-regular tessellation made from squares and octagons. As the semi-regular tessellations emerge students can work out the sizes of the internal angles of the shapes being used.

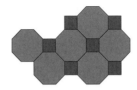

This lesson will work well in a large space such as a hall, so as designs are created they can be left on the floor, perhaps photographed. Alternatively some students might work in another space, a corridor or an adjacent room if available.

Take three triangles

"Triangles appear in a multitude of contexts, from plastic shapes in Early Years Foundation Stage settings to trigonometry and vectors in A-level classrooms."

Make new shapes by joining sides of common length of three triangles formed by dissecting a square by two cuts.

This is another beautifully easy task, which has many possibilities and different depths.

Give each pair of students a copy of the diagram above and ask them to cut out the shapes then form new shapes using the rules:

- Shapes can only be joined by edges of the same length.
- Shapes can be formed using any two triangles or all three triangles.

As shapes are made, some questions to pose are:

- What are the names of the shapes?
- What symmetries do the shapes have?
- If the lengths of the two short sides of triangle A are p and the hypotenuse is q, write the perimeters of the shapes formed in terms of p and q. (The square will have perimeter $4q$.)

Ask students to devise a method to show they have found all possible shapes. Classify the shapes in terms of number of sides and their properties. After some initial exploration about what shapes can be made, organise a discussion about the relative sizes of the triangles, congruence and similarity to enable students to use key vocabulary as they develop the tasks.

Teaching tip

The templates will be easier to work with if they are copied onto card. If you want students to find the symmetries of the shapes it will be easier if the joining lines are not drawn.

Taking it further

Provide those students who are ready to engage with a further challenge with the 'next' size of triangle formed by using two of the larger triangle. How many more shapes can be made? How many sets of similar shapes can be made?

Geoboard I

"If I could take just one resource with me to Mars to demonstrate how I teach mathematics to its inhabitants it would be a square 9-pin geoboard."

The ideas below are all based upon creating shapes using a square 9-pin geoboard and developing concepts of properties, area, perimeter and transformations.

Teaching tip

All the ideas can be carried out using grid paper only. However, there's nowt like the real thing! Making a class set of geoboards from 15 mm block-board (15 cm by 15 cm) and some Escutcheon pins will provide you with a lifetime resource and your students with practical, first-hand experience of the concepts to be explored.

A geoboard is a wooden board with pegs half driven in, around which students can stretch elastic bands to form different shapes. A square 9-pin geoboard has nine pegs in three rows of three.

Give students a geoboard and a selection of elastic bands and ask them to find all the possible non-congruent triangles. Students can then:

- Describe the properties of the triangles and align these to their names.
- Classify the triangles in different ways in terms of equal lengths of sides or right angles. This could lead to drawing Venn diagrams using pairs of criteria of right-angled and two equal sides, scalene and right-angled.
- Find how many congruent triangles there are for each triangle. For example, the triangle in the diagram below can be drawn in eight different places on the grid; this can provide an opportunity for students to engage in the vocabulary of rotation, reflection and translation.

Taking it further

Code the possible lengths as a, (for length 1), b (for length $\sqrt{2}$) and c (for length $\sqrt{5}$) then write the perimeter of each triangle in terms of a, b and c. This will provide students with an elementary experience of collecting like terms.

- Calculate the area of each triangle (assuming the area of one square is 1 unit).
- Measure the perimeter of each triangle (to the nearest mm).

Students who have met Pythagoras' theorem and surds can work out the different possible lengths on a 9-pin board i.e. 1, 2, √2, 2√2 and √5. Students can use this knowledge to determine the perimeter of each triangle.

Bonus idea ★

Extend the task by asking students to find all the possible quadrilaterals or pentagons. Or increase the size of the board to 4 by 4 pins and ask students to find all the triangles and see if they can prove that they have found them all.

Geoboard II

"It is often assumed practical equipment will be eschewed by older, supposedly more sophisticated, KS4 and KS5 students, but many will still play with it given the opportunity."

These ideas are based upon vectors, equations and areas of intersecting shapes.

Make a vector on a 9-dot grid as shown below, and show it to the students.

Then challenge them to work out how many 'different' vectors can be drawn on the grid. Clearly just placing an elastic band on a geoboard does not show its direction so students will need to be careful to add arrows to their diagrams to show directions of travel. You may need to remind students that vectors have both size and direction, so any line should be counted twice.

Mark out a geoboard as a co-ordinate grid, then ask students how many different straight lines are there. Can they describe each line in terms of $y = mx + c$? Can they classify the lines into 'family' types which have the same gradient. For example we can produce a family of three graphs which have a common gradient of 1, i.e. $y = x + 1$, $y = x$ and $y = x - 1$ Other families will have different gradients, for example, -2 etc.

Constructive constructions

"I wanted to find a way for a Year 7 class to learn how to construct shapes using a compass, pencil and ruler without me having to tell them everything in a step-by-step, listen-to-me way."

This idea starts with a jumbled-up set of instructions. Students have to figure out what the correct order is then carry out the instructions. The idea develops to explore other constructions and bisections.

Print the set of instructions below on sheets of card and hand them out to the students. Say that they are instructions to help draw a certain kind of quadrilateral, but unfortunately they have been jumbled up. The first task for the students is to cut out the instructions and rearrange them into a sensible order so that they can be followed.

- Join points C and D with a straight line.
- Open your compasses to 6 cm.
- Mark the ends of the 10 cm length line A and B.
- Draw lines AC, AD and BC.
- Draw a circle with radius 6 cm and the centre at point A.
- Draw a straight line with a ruler 10 cm long.
- Mark one intersection point of the two circles as C and the other as D.
- Draw a circle with radius 6 cm and the centre at point B.

When the students have successfully produced the shape, you can ask some of these questions.

- What kind of shape have you produced?
- Using your protractor, measure just one of the angles then calculate the other angles of the shape without measuring.
- What radii of circles would you need to construct a square?
- Suppose the original line had only been 9 cm long, what radii of circles would you need now to construct a square?

Triangles with constant perimeter

"If students are given investigative, problem-solving ideas from Year 7, lesson 1 they will understand a fundamental basis of mathematics."

How many triangles can be made with integer length sides with a perimeter of 19 cm? This seemingly simple question, about triangles with a constant perimeter, can be developed to many different depths.

Having posed the above question, ask students to work in pairs or a group of three, using A3 sheets of paper to construct triangles with the intention of finding the complete set.

When they think they have gained all possible sets of lengths, encourage students to create a systematic order to check they have not missed any other possible solutions. Ask them to classify triangles according to whether they are scalene, isosceles or equilateral.

For a perimeter (P) of 19 there are ten triangles; five isosceles and five scalene. For P = 18 there are only seven solutions, one of which is equilateral.

Ask students to choose other P values and explore how many different triangles are possible. This is a substantial task, so it is important that students move away from constructing each one to listing all possible triples for their chosen P values. To achieve this they will need to discuss the 'rules' by which a triangle can be formed.

To formalise the rules for constructing a triangle, consider the sides of a scalene triangle, a, b and c; if $a < b < c$ then $a + b > c$.

For an isosceles triangle with sides a, a and b then $2a > b$. Finally there is the equilateral triangle. However this is just a special case of an isosceles triangle, which is defined by having at least two sides of equal length.

What happens if the order of the sides matters? For any scalene triangle there will be six rearrangements (congruencies/solutions), for any isosceles triangle, three and for an equilateral triangle there is just one. Examining the total number of congruencies/solutions gives a most fascinating result.

Extend the idea further by allowing non-integer values. Clearly there will be an infinite set of results, but if students work with a fixed base length then the construction of the loci of an ellipse will not be too far away.

Taking it further

Another challenge is to draw a 'base' length on a co-ordinate grid so the end-points lie on grid points. How can the co-ordinates of the apex be calculated? There are lots of opportunities here to use and apply Pythagoras' theorem as well as to solve simultaneous equations.

Tangrams

"Playing with shapes to form new shapes is both a natural and a very satisfying thing to do. Using play as a purposeful activity is a powerful way to engage learners with mathematics."

This idea is about working with the traditional seven piece tangram set to form polygons; there are 13 possible convex polygons that can be made (where each internal angle is less than 180°). The idea begins with some instructions for students to follow to form the seven pieces.

Teaching tip

Make sure that you have plenty of spare cardboard available, so that students can start again if they cut the wrong shapes.

An interesting way to engage students in the production of the seven tangram pieces is to give a sequence of verbal instructions and see if they can construct the final set of shapes.

- Draw a square ABCD.
- Join B to D.
- Mark the mid-points of AB, AD and BD as points E, F and G.
- Join E to F.
- Draw a line from C through G to EF. Mark the point where the line meets EF as H.
- Mark the mid-point of BG as I, and the mid-point of GD as J.
- Draw a line from E to I, and from H to J.

Taking it further

Use all seven pieces to make the following convex-angled polygons: square, rectangle, isosceles right-angled triangle, trapezium, parallelogram, isosceles trapezium and a hexagon with only two lines of symmetry.

Thousands of different polygons can be formed from the tangram pieces. Ask students to find those that have line symmetry or rotational symmetry of at least order 2.

Denote the length of the small square piece as a (or 1) and the length of the large, overall square as b (or $2\sqrt{2}$), then ask students to find the areas and the perimeters of each individual shape either algebraically or written in surd form.

Bonus idea ★

Ask students if they can find all 13 convex polygons.

An alternative approach is to give students sets of the seven pieces mixed up in envelopes. The first task would be for them to form a square. You may wish to provide the students with an outline so they know the size of square they are being asked to make.

Pentagons from squares

"Creating shapes through paper folding and with or without scissors is a fascinating way of engaging students with geometry."

This idea is based upon a visualisation/mind imagery approach, and can be used to develop students' understanding of line symmetry. The idea develops to consider angles and angle sums of polygons and would be suitable for early KS3 students.

Give each student a square piece of paper and ask them to:

- fold it in half through its vertical line of symmetry to form a rectangle
- cut off an isosceles right-angled triangle from the mid-point of a long side of the rectangle to an opposite top corner.

As a visualisation task, ask students to make a sketch of the shapes they think will be formed before the outcome is revealed. There are two possible outcomes: if you cut from the folded edge you will get a concave pentagon and if you cut from the open edge you will get a convex pentagon.

The idea can be developed in different directions and this will depend upon the main concepts you want students to work on. Some examples are:

- Producing tiling patterns from the different shapes formed.
- Calculating the angle sum of the shapes formed. Helping students make sense of the size of internal angles in concave polygons is an important concept here.

An alternative task is to cut off a scalene right-angled triangle after folding the square by slicing from the mid-point of the long side to the mid-points of each short side.

Teaching tip

KS3 students can measure just one angle of the resulting hexagon and calculate the other angles. KS4 students can use and apply trigonometry to calculate the angles.

Taking it further

Ask students to investigate what happens if a different number of folds is made before slicing a corner off. For example, making a vertical and then a horizontal fold, then cutting off an isosceles right-angled triangle forms an octagon. This is an open-ended investigation that will lead to students discovering patterns for themselves.

Similarity I

"Similarity is a key concept relating to ratio and enlargement."

These ideas require students to follow instructions carefully. They will need some pieces of card, a pencil, a ruler, a compass and scissors.

Give each student a piece of card and ask them to construct two congruent triangles, ABC and LMN, with side lengths AB and LM = 5 cm, BC and MN = 12 cm and AC and LN = 13 cm. Tell them to draw a perpendicular line from side AC to corner B, and mark the point where it meets AC as point D. They should then cut along the line BD.

Students should now have three right-angled triangles: ABD, BCD and LMN. Ask them to examine the triangles and discuss what they notice. They should recognise that each triangle contains the same sizes of angles, which means that they are similar.

Ask students to calculate the scale factors of enlargement between each pair of triangles.

Next ask the students to draw any scalene right-angled triangle ABC, with the right angle at point B, and draw a perpendicular line from corner B to line AC (point D) as before. Can they prove that the three triangles ABC, ABD and BCD are similar?

Similarity II

"Similarity is an interface between multiplicative reasoning and geometry."

These two problems build on students' skills of construction, similarity, ratio and enlargement.

Problem 1: Ask students to construct a triangle PQR with the measurements PQ = 9 cm, PR = 13 cm and QR = 7 cm, and mark a point T on the line PQ that PT = 6 cm. Next, tell them to draw a line TS that is parallel to line QR so that point S is on line PR. Ask the following questions:

- Why are the triangles PQR and PTS are similar?
- What is the ratio of the lengths of sides PT to PQ?
- What are the lengths of sides PS and TS?

Problem 2: Ask students to draw a pair of parallel lines, AB and DE, between 5 cm and 10 cm apart, making the length of AB = 5 cm and the length of DE = 15 cm. They should join the end-points of these lines (A to E and B to D) so they cross over and intersect at point C. The students should now have two triangles, ABC and CDE. Can they prove these two triangles are similar by considering the angles of each triangle? Ask them to check, by measuring, which pairs of sides are in the ratio of 1:3.

The Cairo tessellation

"Offering students practical, hands-on, paper-folding type tasks has the potential to make their learning of mathematics so much more interesting."

This idea is based upon making just one fold in a special size piece of paper and using the resulting polygon to tile the plane.

This design provokes interesting questions about angle sizes and side lengths. The resource is the piece of paper that remains when a square has been cut out from a piece of A4 size paper, i.e. the rectangular shaded piece in the diagram below.

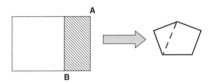

The basic tile is formed by folding corner **A** onto corner **B** – and that's it! The resulting shape is a pentagon which amazingly has four sides of equal length and two 90° angles.

Challenge students to use this tile to fill a 2D space. Use four different colours tiles to help reveal the structure of the design; this also creates a beautiful finished product!

Stuckness

"I've tried everything – now I'm stuck!"

This idea teaches students that stuckness is a state we all get into at times; it should not be seen as a failure or a shortcoming but as a positive state.

This task is about dissecting a defined triangle into smaller triangles; it engages students with important mathematical vocabulary.

Tell students at the outset that your intention is to cause 'stuckness' in order to encourage them to think of ways of getting unstuck and avoid giving up, even if they feel there is no solution. This is all part of developing a classroom culture.

Tell students to dissect an obtuse-angled isosceles triangle into a finite number of acute-angled triangles using straight lines only. Ask them to keep a log/record of the different 'things' they tried/thoughts they had.

Ascertaining that 90° is neither acute nor obtuse is likely to be important information.

There is no 'trickery' involved and the number of acute-angled triangles is finite; there is a very neat geometrical solution.

Teaching tip

Communicating their engagement with mathematics is a powerful way for students to make greater sense of mathematics. Asking them to write a journey of what they did and thought about will enhance their understanding of how they solved the problems above.

Taking it further

Another similar task is to draw any 5-pointed star, and prove that the sum of the angles in the points is 180°.

Dissecting a square

"Roland Sprague first published a dissection of a square into unequal squares in 1939. It used 55 squares."

These ideas are based upon dissecting a square by one, two or more cuts into two or more pieces and considering the properties and areas of new shapes formed and how the shapes can be reformed into a square.

Ask the students to take a square piece of card and cut it from corner to corner. Discuss the shapes and their areas; what observations can the students make?

Proceed by asking the students to make two cuts to a single square. The cuts can be made from a corner to a corner or from the mid-point of an edge to the mid-point of another edge, and cut lines cannot intersect each other. What observations can students make now?

Divide the class into two groups and give different coloured squares to each half, together with paper clips. Invite students to perform a dissection with two or three cuts, but this time all the cuts should intersect. Each student should then paper clip their set of pieces together then swap them with someone who has a different coloured set. Can they reform each other's squares?

Taking it further

For more advanced students, ask them to work out the area of the different shapes they make, assuming that the original square has an area of 1 square unit.

Passola

"It's great to start a lesson with something physical. It gets rid of the twitches."

This idea gets students physically engaged with the shapes they are making.

Ask some students to sit in a circle with their chairs equally spaced and give one student in the circle a ball of string.

Tell the person with the string to hold onto the loose end and pass the ball a fixed number of spaces (the pass size) to someone else in the circle. The person who receives the string should wrap a loop around a finger then pass the ball to another person using the same pass size. This routine continues until the ball of string returns to the first person, at which point a shape, either a polygon, a straight line or a star, will be formed. Students who are not part of the circle can use pre-prepared grid paper to record the shapes.

See what different shapes can be made and talk about how these relate to the number of people in the circle and the pass size used. Encourage students to draw up a two-way table to explain what happens for different numbers of dots on the perimeter and different pass sizes.

Extend the idea by using pairs of pass sizes, for example 2 followed by 1.

Teaching tip

Prepare grid papers in advance with 5, 6, 7, 8, 9, 10, 11, 12, 15 and 16 dots around the perimeters of circles. This should be more than sufficient for students to make conjectures about what is going on.

Taking it further

Ask students to calculate the angles of the vertices of the shapes produced, and to calculate the perimeters.

Enlargements

"Connecting 1D with 2D measures is complex; this needs to be developed carefully and strategically."

This idea uses a co-ordinate grid to explore the relationship between linear and area scale factors under the transformation of enlargement.

Tell students to draw a co-ordinate grid and draw an asymmetric quadrilateral in the first quadrant, ensuring that the four vertices lie on grid points.

Next ask students to calculate the area of their quadrilaterals. Ways to do this include:

- dissecting their shape up into smaller pieces
- framing the shape inside a rectangle, then calculating the difference between the areas of the shapes outside the quadrilateral, but within the rectangle, and the area of the rectangle.

Ask students to double each ordinate and plot the new shape. This will, of course, create an enlargement of the original quadrilateral with the origin as the centre of enlargement. Ask the students to calculate the area of the enlarged shape and compare it with the area of the original.

Repeat this procedure with other quadrilaterals.

Once students have a range of original areas and enlarged areas they can try to work out how the two are connected.

Centres of triangles I

"We throw away so many paper offcuts. There must be something we can do with them."

This idea is based upon using paper folding to work out the centres of triangles, in terms of the inscribed circle, the circumscribed circle and the centre of gravity of a triangle.

These tasks recycle those pieces of sugar paper or card where students have previously cut out a net of a shape right from the middle. The idea here is to cut the waste up into different shaped triangles big enough to do some paper folding with.

The inscribed centre
Give each student a triangle and ask them to fold each angle in half (or bisect each angle). The three fold lines should intersect at a single point. This point is the centre of the inscribed circle which just touches the three sides of the triangle.

The circumscribed centre
Give each student a scalene-angled triangle and ask them to join or fold together pairs of corners. Each of the three folds made becomes the perpendicular bisector of one side and, accuracy allowing, these three lines will intersect at a single point. This point is the centre of a circle that just touches the three corners of the triangle; this is the circumscribed circle.

The centre of gravity or the centroid
Give each student a triangle and ask them to create folds from the mid-point of each edge to each opposite angle. These three lines should intersect at a point and this is the centre of gravity or the centroid; students can check their accuracy by trying to balance their triangle on the end of a pencil at this point of intersection.

Teaching tip

If you join the Association of Teachers of Mathematics you will have access to an amazing archive such as an article by Ruth Eagle in *Mathematics Teaching* 126: www.atm.org.uk/journal/archive/mt126files/ATM-MT126–09-11.pdf.

Taking it further

Ask students to check out the circumscribed centre of triangles which have a right angle or an obtuse angle. Ask students to find the orthocentre of a triangle. This is created by 'dropping a perpendicular' from each corner to its opposite side.

Centres of triangles II

"As students develop their mathematical thinking they can be introduced to a range of different 'centres' of triangles."

This idea is about using both drawing and IT skills to make sense of the different centres of circles.

Technical drawing skills such as forming triangles, carrying out angle and line bisections and dividing a line up into any number of equal segments can empower students, as well as giving them pleasure from the beauty of geometric constructions.

The intention is for students to develop the construction skills of drawing triangles, bisecting angles and bisecting lines. The traditional way of finding the inscribed and circumscribed centres of triangles is to construct them using compass, pencil and a straight edge.

Exploring Euler's line

This is the connection between the circumscribed circle centre, the centre of gravity (or the centroid) and the orthocentre.

This problem requires the following construction:

- draw a circle and mark three points A, B, C 'widely' (though not equally) spaced on the circumference of the circle
- join these points together to form triangle ABC
- draw tangents to the circle at each point A, B, C.

Where these tangents intersect each other (in pairs) mark points P, Q, R

We now have two triangles, ABC and PQR. The challenge is to find relationships between the angles in triangle ABC and the angles in triangle PQR.

Find the radius of the inscribed circle for a triangle with lengths 3, 4, 5.

What about a triangle with lengths 5, 12, 13?

Explore for other Pythagorean triples, which are right-angled triangles with integer length sides, so the next one begins with a length 7, but what are the length of the other two sides?

To develop this idea, what about the radius of the Pythagorean triple 8, 15, 17.

What are the next few Pythagorean triple with an even smallest value? (Be careful to avoid enlargements of the previous set of triples, for example, 6, 8, 10 which is just an enlargement of 3, 4, 5.)

Taking it further

Using software such as *Cabri Géomètre*, *Autograph* or *GeoGebra* will help them develop geometric thinking and move towards generality.

Secret squares

"Squares can be represented as an arithmetical calculation, a 2D geometrical shape, the 2 in cm², a face on a 3D shape or someone who used to be described as not being 'cool'."

This idea is about seeking out centres of rotation between two squares and coming to recognise the geometrical relationship between these centres and the centres of the squares themselves.

Give students some grid paper and tell them to shade two squares as shown.

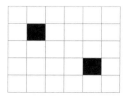

- Ask students to find different centres of rotation so that one square can be rotated exactly on top of the other square (there is more than one centre to be found). Join these centres of rotation together and see what happens.
- What happens if the two squares lie in the same horizontal or vertical plane?

Get the students to challenge each other by setting their own problems. If they are given just one square and some centres of rotation that will transform this square onto another 'secret' square, can they find the position of the secret square without performing a rotation?

Co-ordinated transformations

"In the previous century transformational geometry came to the fore and Euclidean geometry went into decline ... thank goodness we are now paying equal attention to both of these aspects of geometry."

This idea is about exploring transformations using a co-ordinate grid.

Ask students to plot an asymmetric quadrilateral $A_0 B_0 C_0 D_0$ on a co-ordinate grid and write the co-ordinates of the points A_0, B_0, C_0 and D_0. Then ask them to multiply each x-ordinate by minus 1 and each y-ordinate by 1 to form the quadrilateral $A_1 B_1 C_1 D_1$. Can they tell you what transformation has taken place?

Challenge the students to find out what happens under the following sets of conditions.

- Multiply each x-ordinate by 1 and each y-ordinate by -1 to form $A_2 B_2 C_2 D_2$.
- Multiply each x-ordinate by -1 and each y-ordinate by -1 to form $A_3 B_3 C_3 D_3$.
- Swap the co-ordinates so (x, y) becomes (y, x) to form $A_4 B_4 C_4 D_4$.
- Multiply each x-ordinate by 1 and each y-ordinate by -1 then swap the co-ordinates to form $A_5 B_5 C_5 D_5$.
- Multiply each x-ordinate by -1 and each y-ordinate by 1 then swap the co-ordinates to form $A_6 B_6 C_6 D_6$.
- Multiply each x-ordinate by -1 and each y-ordinate by -1 then swap the co-ordinates to form $A_7 B_7 C_7 D_7$.

Students should determine the transformations that have taken place each time, starting from $A_0 B_0 C_0 D_0$.

Choose other pairs of shapes, such as $A_1 B_1 C_1 D_1$ to $A_5 B_5 C_5 D_5$, and ask students to determine the transformation from the first to the second.

Teaching tip

Tracing paper will be a useful resource for students to have access to.

Taking it further

Ask students to explore what happens when they carry out pairs of transformations using their tracing paper, always beginning from their original quadrilateral. For example, what happens if they rotate the quadrilateral by $90°$ clockwise around the origin, then reflect (by turning their tracing paper over) in the x-axis (or the $y = 0$ line).

Bonus idea ★

Ask students to draw up a two-way table to capture all possible transformations from every shape to every other shape. This may need to be a team effort!

Co-ordinated lines

"Tracing paper makes it easy to visualise the different transformations."

This idea explores how the equations of straight lines change under transformations of reflection, rotation and translation.

Teaching tip

This is an extension task for students who are comfortable with the concept that a straight line has the general equation $y = mx + c$.

Give students a co-ordinate grid and a sheet of tracing paper. Ask them to put the tracing paper on top of the grid and draw a straight line. The gradient of the line should not be 0, 1, −1 or infinite (i.e. the line is neither horizontal, vertical, nor inclined at 45° or 135°), and the y-intercept should not be 0. Tell students to write the equation of the starting line, for example, $y = 2x + 3$.

Next ask the students to rotate the tracing paper anticlockwise through 90° about (0, 0). Can they find the equation of the new line? How does it compare to the equation of the original?

Taking it further

Explore what happens when the original line is reflected in $y = 0$, $x = 0$, $y = x$ and $y = -x$.

Invite them to return the line to its original place then rotate it anticlockwise through 270° about (0, 0). How does the equation of the new line compare with the original now? What happens if the original line is rotated through 180°?

More co-ordinate problems

"I like it when we can set our own problems for each other. It makes the lesson more interesting."

These ideas are based upon a sequence of problems where students have to find certain points according to different conditions and then seek generalities.

Ask students to find the mid-point of the straight line segment between points (2, 5) and (6, 3), then do lots of similar examples choosing different pairs of starting points. Can students generalise for the mid-point between any two points P_1 and P_2? Does their generality holds when negative ordinates are used?

Tell students to work in pairs. Each student should draw some squares on a co-ordinate grid and write the co-ordinates of the corners of the squares, then give their partner information about two points for each square. This might be a pair of adjacent points (in which case there will be two solutions) or a pair of diagonally opposite points (in which case there will be a unique solution). Can the partners draw the squares from the information provided?

Once they have drawn the squares, they can work together to find the area of each square.

Teaching tip

In setting up each task there are, potentially, two important issues. The first is teacher expectation, that students are able to generate examples for themselves and for each other. The second is ownership, of students developing a task without the teacher needing to prepare a worksheet.

Bonus idea ★

In pairs, each student draws a pentagon with three right angles and one line of symmetry. Students have to determine what the minimum information is which they can give their partner so they reproduce each other's pentagons.

Information could be taken from combinations of:

- the equation of the line of symmetry
- the area of the pentagon
- one, two or three co-ordinates of the corners
- the co-ordinates of mid-points of some of the sides
- the equations of some of the lines which form the pentagon.

Co-ordinates and vectors

"Pythagoras' theorem is yet another fascinating aspect of mathematics to introduce students to."

These ideas build on problems described in *More co-ordinate problems*. The purpose is for students to see how the system of co-ordinates relates to the system of vectors.

Tell students to mark two points, A and B, on a square grid and record their co-ordinates. Then ask them to draw the line segment AB and describe AB in vector format. For any two points A (x_1, y_1) and B (x_2, y_2), can they determine the vectors AB and BA?

If P_1 and P_2 are adjacent corners of a square, challenge students to find points P_3 and P_4 such that P_1, P_2, P_3 and P_4 form a square (there are two solutions to this problem). Discuss the four vectors formed between pairs of adjacent corners of the square, and try to generalise.

If P_1 and P_3 are opposite corners of a square P_1, P_2, P_3, P_4, can students find points P_2 and P_4? Again, discuss the vectors formed between opposite corners of the square and relate these to the vectors formed between adjacent corners, and try to generalise.

Tell students to work out the area of a number of squares and write one of the vectors formed between a pair of adjacent corners for each square. Can they find a connection between the area and the chosen vector for each square? Can they generalise their findings?

Circular geoboards I

"Even older students enjoy playing with geoboards and elastic bands. Watch out for those who like to flick the bands though!"

If you've already used a square geoboard, introducing a circular one will provide students with a different challenge.

Use a circular geoboard with 9 equally spaced pins on the circumference and one at the centre, and pose the problem of finding and recording as many 'different' (non-congruent) triangles as possible. Corners of the triangles can and cannot touch the centre pin.

Ask some students to record one each of the shapes they have made on the board/screen. This will create opportunities to:

- classify the triangles
- discuss congruence
- describe the shapes.

Ask the students to try to prove that they have found all the possible triangles. This will cause them to think and work systematically.

Encourage students to give clear explanations by asking them to describe the shape as 'over a telephone'. This is so that students use verbal instructions to consider ways of codifying shapes.

Circular geoboards II

"Learners have to re-interpret what is offered and make sense of it for themselves. This is what it means to say that learning is an active process." (Wigley 1992, p6)

This idea follows naturally from *Circular geoboards I*. The task is to explore angle sizes.

Teaching tip

As suggested by the article *Models for Teaching Mathematics*, from which the quote above is taken, you may wish to be circumspect about doing too much 'path-smoothing'.

Students will need to have a complete collection of triangles that can be made on a 9-pin (on the circumference) board. Encourage them to record the triangles they have produced in a systematic way, so that they can work through them.

Challenge students to calculate the sizes of the angles of each triangle. They should write clear explanations to show how they calculated the sizes.

Calculating angles can be something of a challenge. Starting by working out the angles of the triangles that have a corner at the centre pin will smooth the path.

Taking it further

Ask students to make and codify all different triangles made on 10 and 12 pin grids, and calculate the sizes of angles of these triangles.

A further extension task could be for students to explore how many different triangles are possible for circular geoboards with different numbers of pins on the circumference (+1 at the centre). For example there are four possible triangles on a 5 (+1) pin grid whereas on a 9 (+1) grid there are 11 possible triangles.

Circular geoboards III

"The idea of angle is a fundamental geometrical concept." (French 2004)

These ideas are a stepping stone for developing students' understanding of angle and circle theorems.

The two triangles below are drawn with a common side AB.

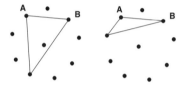

Challenge students to draw other, non-congruent triangles which have a common side AB, and compare the sizes of the opposite angles. Extend the work by considering the angles of triangles made on 10 or 12 pin grids with one side a diameter.

Invite students to make or draw some quadrilaterals whose vertices all lie on the circumference. These will be cyclic quadrilaterals and by examining the angles students can begin to recognise that opposite angles in a cyclic quadrilateral sum to 180°.

Tell the students to make or draw some quadrilaterals where one of the corners lies on the centre pin. This will produce two possible scenarios. If a chevron shape is made then the outside angle at the centre will be twice the opposite angle at the circumference. If any other quadrilateral is formed then there is another interesting connection to be found between the internal angle at the centre and the opposite angle at the circumference.

Teaching tip

It is important for students to recognise that although the solutions to these problems demonstrate certain facts about angle/circle theorems, they are not proofs.

Bonus idea

These ideas are a further opportunity for students to use and apply their knowledge of Pythagoras and trigonometry.

Returning to the triangles previously made, ask students to calculate their perimeters. Whether (or if) students need to be reminded it would be a 'good' idea to describe the length from the centre pin to any outside pin as unit length is clearly a decision for individual teachers to make.

Ask students to calculate the area of the triangles they have found. This will require them to delve even deeper into their trigonometric knowledge banks.

3D Geometry problems

Part 4

Using ATM MATs I

"MATs are an amazing resource, sold by the Association of Teachers of Mathematics and created by Adrian Pinel. Using small amounts of Copydex glue, MATs can be used to make all kinds of solids."

This idea is based upon students working, in the first instance, with equilateral triangle MATs only. The intention is for students to create solids within this parameter.

Using equilateral triangle MATs it is possible to create a set of solids called the deltahedra. There are eight such solids, three of which are Platonic solids: the tetrahedron, the octahedron and the icosahedron. Finding the other five will require students to shift their thinking away from designing shapes which are multi-symmetric.

The names of the remaining five deltahedra are anything other than straightforward, but can be found in Cundy and Rollett, *Mathematical Models* (Tarquin Publications, 1981).

When students have created their solids, ask them to count how many faces (*F*), vertices (*V*) and edges (*E*) each has and explore how these are connected together by Euler's rule.

Using ATM Mats II

"The most suitable, and in many ways the most attractive, subject for an experiment in the construction of mathematical models is a set of polyhedra."

Having explored solids made from only equilateral triangles in *Using ATM MATs I*, the work continues to find the remaining two Platonic solids, to explore the relationship between the tetrahedron and the octahedron and to consider the symmetries of these polyhedra.

Students will need to have access to the tetrahedron, the octahedron and the icosahedron made previously. To complete the set of the Platonic solids, which are defined by solids made from regular polygons where each vertex is formed by the same number of shapes, students will need squares and pentagons.

Having made the five Platonic solids students can check that the faces, edges and vertices of these solids conform to Euler's rule.

The next idea is to consider symmetries, in terms of plane (mirror) symmetry and axes of symmetry (order of rotational).

One way to define plane symmetry is to consider how a solid can be sliced into two congruent pieces. For a cube (hexahedron) there are three planes of symmetry, each one 'slicing' through four faces and producing two cuboids. You can also slice along an edge, diagonally through two faces, and through a second edge as shown in the diagram opposite. Ask students to draw what the resulting congruent pair of solids would look like.

Teaching tip

ATM MATs can be joined together using a small amount of Copydex. Because of the elasticised nature of this glue it can easily be peeled off so that solids can be recycled and used again.

Taking it further

Ask students to make solids using combinations of square and equilateral triangles. Some examples are:

- a triangular prism
- a square-based anti-prism
- a cuboctahedron made from 6 squares and 8 equilateral triangles.

Challenge KS4 or KS5 students to prove that there are just five Platonic solids.

Truncations and duals

"The magic, the beauty and the many connections between polyhedra is a rich area of mathematics for students to explore."

This idea is for students to explore the truncations of the five Platonic solids, i.e. the tetrahedron, hexahedron, octahedron, icosahedron and dodecahedron.

There are two different types of truncation. One is to slice off the vertices of a solid through the mid-point of the edges that meet at each vertex. The other is to slice off the vertices through a point somewhere between the vertex and the mid-point (for example, one third of the distance down each edge). These truncations are referred to as types A and B, respectively.

A type A truncation of a tetrahedron creates an octahedron. This may come as no surprise to students who worked on the idea from *Using ATM MATs II* but it is, nevertheless, a fascinating introduction to truncations. In order to set the scene, ask students to record the number of faces, edges and vertices for a solid and its truncations; this is not to check that they conform to Euler but so they get into the habit of gathering data for analysis.

Working in small groups students can explore type A and B truncations for each of the Platonic solids. Using their ten pieces of data of the type A and B truncations for the five Platonic solids, students can look for connections between each solid and its truncations.

Linking cubes I

"Another manipulative that provides opportunities for students to have first-hand experience with mathematics."

These problems are all based on creating then exploring solids, beginning with cuboids, from a given number of linking cubes.

Give pairs of students 24 cubes and ask them to use all of them to create cuboids. There will be a fixed number of solutions; asking students to prove they have found the complete set will require them to consider the divisors of 24.

Once a complete set has been found some further tasks are:

- sketch their solutions on isometric-dot paper
- determine the surface areas of the cuboids
- arrange them in order from minimum to maximum
- discuss why the surface areas are different (this should cause students to consider dimensions).

Without using linking cubes ask students to visualise how many different cuboids can be made using, say, 48 cubes. If the cuboid were made from Plasticine what would be the dimensions and, therefore, the surface area for a volume of 48 cubic units?

Ask students to explore what they do with the dimensions in order to determine each cuboid's surface area. This clearly leads to a generality, so students determine how to derive the formulae for the surface area of a cuboid if they know the dimensions are a, b and c.

Teaching tip

Drawing 3D shapes on isometric paper is a skill some students can do intuitively while others require support to help them become confident. You might make use of the teaching strategy where students who can help those who cannot. However, being able to represent 3D shapes in a 2D picture is only a means to an end to solving deeper problems.

Taking it further

You can reverse this idea: starting with a known surface area of 100 square units, if the dimensions are positive integers, what could the dimensions be? While this appears to be a trial and improvement type question, it can be worked on systematically if students take into account their derived surface area formula.

IDEA 76

Linking cubes II

"Sometimes the problems that seem the simplest have interesting stings in their tails."

This set of ideas is based upon creating structures from just four cubes.

Teaching tip

Having access to an isometric-dot grid on the interactve whiteboard (IWB) would be very useful.

Taking it further

The 'Soma Cube' is a famous puzzle consisting of six of the possible structures made from four cubes, along with a further structure containing just three cubes. In total this makes 27 cubes. The challenge is to make a 3 by 3 by 3 cube using these seven structures.

Using four linking cubes, ask students to find all the different shapes by joining them together and drawing their solutions. Discounting rotations there are less than a dozen possible solutions. Organise a discussion about what 'different' means in relation to the shapes to highlight that two of the solutions are a reflection of one another. However, they are considered different because the shapes cannot be orientated so they would fit into the same frame (of just four cubes).

Ask the students to determine:

- what symmetries each shape possesses
- what different surface areas the shapes have.

Ask students to prove they have found a complete set of shapes.

If a whole-class approach to this question is felt desirable, this problem might be a useful context for engaging all the students in discussions about the notion of proof. One approach might be to invite individuals to draw their solutions on the screen and use the collection of results to discuss how a proof of completeness might be developed.

Alternative net

"Sometimes I want to provide a class with a 'closed' puzzle, designed to grab interest and give them something to think about."

This is a one-off type idea, about cutting out a shape containing eight squares then folding it up to make a cube.

Ask the students follow these instructions.

1 Divide a square piece of card equally into nine small squares arranged in a 3 by 3 grid. Before starting, make sure that one side of the paper is shaded and one side is not.
2 Cut through from any one of the lines that go from the edge towards the middle. Continue this cut around the centre square.
3 Throw this away centre square away.
4 You now have a shape with eight squares in a 'ring' separated by one cut. Score the remaining seven joins between the eight remaining squares.
5 Now try to form a cube by folding up the eight squares.

Can students find all possible solutions, which have different numbers of shaded and non-shaded faces for the cubes?

Teaching tip

An enlarged version of the diagram can be given to students, who then need to cut along the thick black line to gain the required shape containing eight squares (joined at seven edges).

Bonus idea

Make the task more complex by asking students to explain verbally and/or diagrammatically how the problem can be solved. To record different solutions students might code all the squares on one side as 1, 2, . . . 8 and all the squares on the other side as A, B, . . . H.

Cube dissection I

"Inside every cube is a tetrahedron just waiting to get out."

This idea dissects a cube into four congruent equilateral triangular-based pyramids and a tetrahedron.

Begin by constructing a right-angled isosceles triangle. Draw an equilateral triangle on the hypotenuse of the right-angled isosceles triangle then draw two further isosceles right-angled triangles on the remaining two sides of the equilateral triangle. This will be the net of a square-based pyramid. Transfer your construction onto card and cut this out; not forgetting, of course, to draw flaps on three of the six equal edges of the newly formed shape. This will be your template net.

You will now need a further three of these nets so you have four equilateral triangle-based pyramids in total.

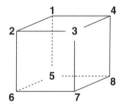

The apices of these four pyramids are going to be four of the eight corners of the cube, for example, corners 1, 3, 6 and 8.

The tetrahedron is the same size as the four equilateral triangle faces of the four pyramids. This is a relatively easy net to make as shown on the diagram below, together with flaps.

The pyramids and the tetrahedron can now be put together to form a cube.

Taking it further

Make eight of the pyramids and join them together to make an octahedron. This can lead to the construction of formulae (where T = Tetrahedron, C = Cube, P = Pyramid and O = Octahedron), for example: C = 4P + T, 8P = O. Ask students to write an equation connecting C with O.

Bonus idea ★

Once you have made the octahedron make four tetrahedra and explore how these five solids can be used to form an even larger tetrahedron. There is, subsequently, the possibility of working out the ratio of the volume of the octahedron to the volume of the tetrahedron; visually this provides a most surprising result.

Cube dissection II

"3D geometry is fascinating and the connections between the solids are amazing."

This idea shows how a cube can be dissected into six congruent square-based pyramids.

Invite students to construct six square-based pyramids with a perpendicular height (between the centre of the base and the apex) of half the length of the side of the base. How much guidance you give them in the construction of the pyramids will depend upon their abilities and experience.

Students can then form a cube by joining the six pyramids by their square base edges.

To extend the idea, ask students to wrap the square faces of the six square-based pyramids around another cube and see what the resulting solid looks like. This is called a rhombic dodecahedron.

Students can join several of the rhombic dodecahedra together to reveal another fascinating property: the solids will fill the 3D plane without any gaps.

Measurement problems

Part 5

Cuboids I

"Algebra needs to permeate mathematics, to be used and applied as a tool for making sense of and solving problems."

This task starts with rectangular pieces of paper and moves on to producing cuboids. It lends itself to the use and application of algebra.

Instruct students to take two rectangular pieces of paper both measuring 20 cm by 28 cm. They should fold one piece lengthways into four equally wide strips (each being 7 cm), open up then refold into an open-ended cuboid; call this exhibit A.

This should be repeated with the other piece of paper, but this time fold it widthways into four 5 cm wide strips; as before make a cuboid and call this exhibit B. Both will be open-ended cuboids.

Ask students to calculate the volumes each cuboid will hold. Which has the largest volume? Why?

If the students were to make tops and bases for each cuboid, what would their surface areas be?

Ask the students to calculate the volumes and surface areas that would be generated, without folding, if the same idea were repeated starting with two pieces of paper with dimensions 18 cm by 30 cm.

Now ask them to choose their own set of dimensions and calculate the volume and surface areas of the resulting cuboids. What would happen if the paper were square?

Geoboard III

"So many problems can be posed using geoboards!"

This idea uses a square 9-pin geoboard as a context for students to use and apply trigonometric ratios.

Pose the question: 'How many different angles can be drawn on a 9-dot grid and what are their sizes?' This is a very simple problem to pose, yet students will need to draw upon and use their knowledge of trigonometry to solve it. Assume that the shortest length between adjacent points is 1.

For an angle such as the one marked below, because it is not an angle within a right-angled triangle, students would need to add some construction lines. The diagram shows some (dotted) construction lines to create a right-angled triangle, which now contains the angle under exploration.

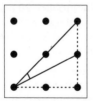

Teaching tip

The method of adding construction lines is perhaps the key to unlocking this problem; your challenge as a teacher is to see how long you are prepared to let the students try to overcome any 'stuckness' before offering this clue!

Taking it further

An obvious task to provide further practise and consolidation opportunities is to pose the same problem on a 16-dot square grid.

Angle folding I

"Origami, or paper folding can, at its simplest, provides an amazing amount of mathematics to be worked on . . . simple starting points with lots of extension possibilities."

This idea looks at how a few simple folds in a piece of A4 paper can open up a range of further tasks centred on understanding angles.

Give each student a piece of A4 paper and instruct them to make three folds as follows.

- Fold the paper in half lengthways, and open it out again.
- With a short edge at the bottom, fold the bottom right corner (B) up to meet the first fold line, with the new fold line going through the bottom left corner (A).
- Without opening out the second fold, make a third fold that runs along the short edge that has been folded up.

These three folds produce 20 angles, including three of the original right angles. Because angle A has been trisected, it is possible for all the angles to be calculated.

Ask students to state what angle facts they have used to calculate the angles; this will cause them to become explicit about what they have done implicitly.

Bonus idea ★

If you label each corner, and each point where a fold meets an edge or another fold, you can identify a range of different sided polygons. Having identified lots of pentagons, ask students to calculate the angle sum for each one. Students who have made the fourth fold line to bisect angle B will have access to polygons with even more sides, an 11 sided polygon. Armed with this information, students can look for the connection between the number of sides and the angle sum of a polygon.

Angle folding II

"Powerful ideas in mathematics can be gleaned from simple starting points."

This task starts with angle calculations and finishes with algebraic descriptions of the angles previously calculated.

Label the rectangle ABCD.

Draw or fold a line EF which goes from one side to the side opposite.

Draw/fold a second line GH which joins the other two sides together.

I intentionally avoid these two lines from intersecting at right-angles.

Ask student to measure one angle where the lines cross and a second angle where one of the lines meets the edge of the paper.

Without any further measuring it is now possible to calculate the other ten angles, assuming the four corner angles are 90° each.

Taking it further

Draw/fold a third line, JM, which is perpendicular to one of the other two lines, in this example to EF.

There are eight further angles to be calculated, excluding the four right-angles at point K

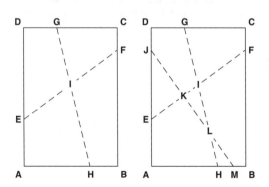

Bonus idea ★

By replacing the two angles initially measured, with α and β ask students to work out the sizes of all the other angles, apart from the right-angles, in terms of α and β.

Area of 20 cm²

"Mathematical understanding is enhanced by multiple representations."

This idea offers students opportunities to develop their understanding of the concept of the area of a rectangle beyond the simplistic, formulaic notion of 'length multiplied by width'.

Challenge students to find all the rectangles on a square grid with an area of 20 cm², such that the corners of the rectangle always lie on grid points.

There are three 'easy' solutions: 1 by 20, 2 by 10 and 4 by 5. There are four more solutions, none of which are congruent rectangles to the three listed. One of the solutions is arrived at by the calculation $(1^2 + 3^2)$ x 2, or the sum of two square numbers multiplied by 2, but what does the picture look like?

When 20 cm² has been exhausted, the following areas will provide students with much to think about: 50 cm², 72 cm², 90 cm² and 100 cm². Each of these has a minimum of nine solutions.

Area of a trapezium

"Deriving formulae via an investigative approach so students know how, why and where such formulae have been constructed supports deep learning."

This investigative approach is designed to help students understand the formula for the area of a trapezium.

Ask students to each draw a trapezium on 2 cm squared grid paper and calculate its area in terms of the number of squares (rather than its actual area in square centimetres). The area value should be written inside each trapezium.

Ask students to cut out their trapezia and stick them onto one or two sheets of sugar paper with sticky tack. This instant display will provide the information for students to investigate.

With the poster(s) exhibited on the board, ask students to discuss, initially in pairs, anything they notice about the set of trapezia and their areas. What information about the trapezia might they consider in order to be able to calculate the area, beyond counting squares?

If students have been brought up on a diet of looking for patterns and seeking connections, you should expect some of their discussions to focus on the dimensions of the shapes. If students have not been challenged to think mathematically then a more directed approach might be necessary.

Draw students attention to the fact that trepezia with the same length parallel sides and perpendicular height have the same area, even if they look like very different shapes.

Teaching tip

The reason for using 2 cm square grid paper is so the diagrams can be seen easily. Use felt pens to draw the trapezia and to write the area (number of squares). Making instant, working posters is an excellent way of providing students with data to investigate.

Taking it further

Find a way of calculating the area (A) of any trapezium in terms of its parallel sides, a and b, and its perpendicular height, h, and try to write a formula for A in terms of a, b and h.

Square triangles

"Pythagoras' theorem is based upon an equality . . . but what does $a^2 + b^2 > c^2$ look like?"

This idea is based upon students exploring different types of scalene triangles formed when surrounded by three squares.

Students will need 15 squares measuring from 3 cm² to 17 cm². They should choose three squares and use an edge of each square to form or 'surround' triangles. Because of the lengths chosen there will be many sets of three squares that will not form triangles; this can lead to students recognising that the total length of the two shorter sides needs to be greater than the longest side in order to form a triangle.

Working in pairs or a small group ask students to calculate the area of each square and write it on the square. The two main points are for students to explore:

- which sets of lengths will make scalene triangles
- the areas of squares which 'surround' scalene triangles classified as all acute angles, one obtuse angle and one right angle.

The lengths used can generate between 200 and 250 scalene triangles; given that just five of the triangles will be right-angled, students will have a substantial challenge to find these triangles. This lends itself to a whole-class activity, working in groups to systematically seek out the five right-angled solutions.

The focus of Pythagoras' theorem is based upon the equality $a^2 + b^2 = c^2$. What kind of triangles satisfy the conditions $a^2 + b^2 < c^2$ and $a^2 + b^2 > c^2$?

Circles I

"Making sense of mathematics is fundamental to students becoming more confident more competent problem-solvers."

It is not easy for students to make sense of the formula $C = \pi d$, where C is the circumference and d is the diameter of a circle, yet it is most important. This idea is based upon students working with strips of (scrap) paper of different lengths to generate the formula for themselves.

Ask students to follow these instructions.

- Take a strip of paper and measure its length to the nearest millimetre.
- Join the two ends together with sticky tape without any overlap so the previous measure is the circumference of the circle.
- Roll a finger of each hand around the inside of the strip to form a shape as close as possible to a circle.
- Measure the diameter of the circle.
- Record the two measurements (circumference and diameter).
- Repeat these steps for a number of different length strips.

Set up a spreadsheet on the IWB so that students can input their data and analyse it to look for an approximate connection between the circumferences and the diameters.

If any odd data appears on the spreadsheet the students can check these out.

The crux issue is for students to recognise when the circumference is divided by something close to 3 this gives the diameter. This might be achieved by setting up another column in the spreadsheet to calculate $C \div d$. In addition the mean average for $C \div d$ can also be calculated and recorded on the spreadsheet.

Teaching tip

Lead a class discussion to explore all the connections between the measurements of a circle: circumference to diameter and diameter to circumference, circumference to radius and so on. This may appear obvious, but it is important for students to become fluent with the inverse relationships as this supports their understanding of the associated formulae and is an important part of gaining a deeper understanding.

Taking it further

Ask students to draw a graph of C against d, to help them recognise the connection. If they graph the multiples of three on the same pair of axes, students may recognise a similarity between the two graphs.

Circles II

"The circle is a fascinating geometric connector to number, algebra and statistical representation."

This idea allows students to become familiar with and form connections, both algebraically and graphically, between pairs of symbols C, d, r (radius), A (area) and the constant π.

Circles I involved drawing a graph of C against d in order to show the approximate relationship $C = 3d$. Prior to this lesson, ask students to find out what they can about the symbol π and the formula for the area of a circle. At the beginning of the next lesson, organise a discussion where students can share what they have found and what they understand.

Having this fact out in the open is one thing, but the next step is to demonstrate the approximate truth that $A = \pi r^2$. To do this, ask students to each draw one circle, on 1 cm squared paper, taken from a list of different radii between 3 cm and 10 cm. Ask them to choose a value with one decimal place such as 5.7 cm. Having drawn their circle they should calculate its area by counting whole and part squares.

Again, set up a spreadsheet and ask students to input their data in columns headed r and A. As the data appears they can start to check the reasonableness of their circle area when the formula is applied.

Making another column in the spreadsheet containing the formulae $A = \pi r^2$ will provide a further checking mechanism.

Prism volume

"There are prisms and anti-prisms and both are infinite sets of Archimedean solids."

This idea involves collecting data regarding the volume of prisms with different numbers of base edges and seeing what happens to the volume as the number of base edges increases.

Provide each pair of students with six pieces of A5 size card and ask them to fold one each into 3, 4, 5, 6 and 8 equal columns, with the card in a landscape orientation. They should then fold each piece of card into the shape of a prism, using a strip of sticky tape to join the two end edges together. Obviously, for five columns a pentagonal prism will be formed. The sixth piece of paper should be formed into a cylinder.

By placing the base of each prism on 1 cm square grid paper, ask students to calculate the area of each base by counting squares. Given that the height of each prism will be the same, 21 cm, the volume of each prism can be calculated and compared.

Ask students to estimate the volume of a prism that has a seven-sided base. Consider successive percentage increases in volume as the numbers of sides of the bases increase from three to eight sides.

Teaching tip

This task will be more suited to KS3 students. However the same idea can also be used with older students by expecting them to use and apply their knowledge of trigonometry and the area of a circle to calculate the volumes of the prisms more accurately.

Taking it further

Plot a graph of volume against number of sides. Can they form a pattern?

Beans, beans, beans

"There's a whole lot of mathematics to be had from a tin of beans . . . we just need a few questions to go alongside it."

This idea is about whether a normal size tin of beans has an optimal surface area for a given volume.

Pass two or three (identical) tins of beans around the class, requesting students only keep hold of a can for at most ten seconds. Then ask them to write a secret estimate of the volume they think one of the tins holds. Collect the data and do some statistics with their estimates.

Next ask students to write a (secret) estimate of the surface area of the tin. Repeat as above. These are two open scenarios.

Alternatively, ask students to calculate the volume and surface area, to two significant figures, if the radius is 3.65 cm and the height is 10.5 cm. Then consider the following.

- Starting with the equation for the volume of a cylinder $V = \pi r^2 h$, ask students to search out pairs of values for r and h to satisfy the equation $\pi r^2 h = 440$.
- Having gathered, say, a dozen or so different pairs of values the next step is to determine what the surface area of the tin would be for these pairs of values.

What is the percentage difference between the surface area of the commercial product and the minimum it could be?

Practical tangents

"Discussing what the phrase 'Going off at a tangent' means can be an interesting start to working on this concept."

In this idea students create a table of tangents, without initially realising what they are doing.

Provide students with 2 cm squared grid paper and ask them to draw five or six right-angled triangles, keeping to the grid lines in the first instance.

Set up a spreadsheet and ask students to fill in pieces of information as they complete their different diagrams and measures, as indicated below:

opposite length	adjacent length	Measured angle	The ratio $o{:}a$ as a fraction	The ratio $o{:}a$ as a decimal
3	5	31°	3/5	0.6
5	2	68°	5/2	2.5
1	3	18°	1/3	0.333
3	4	37°	3/4	0.75
3	2	56°	3/2	1.5

Once the spreadsheet has, say, upwards of 20 columns ask students to discuss, perhaps in pairs or a group of three, anything they notice about the data.

Questions to help direct the discussion are:

- What happens to the ratio between the 'opposite' and 'adjacent' sides as the angle increases?
- What happens to the angle as the ratio increases?
- What is special about those angles whose ratio is 1?
- What happens as the measured angle approaches 90°?

Teaching tip

Asking students to make posters to explain what they have been doing, and what they have found out and understood, is one way of helping them become explicit about their learning.

Taking it further

Ask students to use the TAN key on their calculators followed by the measured angles and add this data in an extra column on the right-hand side of the table. Discuss the closeness of their answers in the ratio and the TAN columns. Of course if there are any anomalies these can also be checked for accuracy.

Bonus idea ★

Lead students in exploring what happens to the ratio $a{:}o$ for the TAN of angles greater than 90° and less than 180°? What does the graph of angle plotted against the decimal ratio look like?

Circular functions I

"Trigonometric functions are circular functions and as such the unit circle is an essential image for students to have in order to make sense of sine and cosine."

This idea focuses on students creating sine and cosine tables without realising, in the initial stages, that this is what they are doing.

To begin the process of understanding sine and cosine students need only understand the following three concepts:

1 angle is a measure of turn
2 a line of length 1 can be divided into ten equal (decimal) parts
3 how to read co-ordinates.

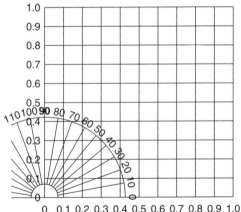

Give each student a copy of the rotating arm grid. The size of the grid is irrelevant but it must be square. Give students the following instructions.

• Draw a line 1 unit long from (0, 0) through the 10° line shown by the protractor.

- Read off the co-ordinates of the end point of this line, writing answers to two decimal places.
- Record results in a table with columns angle, *x*-ordinate and *y*-ordinate.
- Repeat this procedure for 20°, 30° etc. all the way up to 90°.

Once students have completed the task of reading off the *x*- and *y*-ordinates for angles from 0° to 90° (going up in 10°), they can use their information for the following questions.

- Look carefully at the information and write down anything you notice. What is going on here?
- At what angle do you think both ordinates will be equal? Why do you think this is?
- Without drawing any lines, use your information to estimate the *x*- and *y*-ordinates for the following angles: 63°, 27°, 18°, 72°. What do you notice about your answers? What is going on here?

Circular functions II

"An important part of learning is about practising routines but first of all students need to know where these routines come from and why they work."

This idea continues from *Circular functions I* and assumes that all students have, as a minimum, a completed table of values on which they have carried out some analysis.

Teaching tip

In addition to thinking about right-angled triangles students can also write the calculations they carry out as 'calculator sequences', by drawing each button they press when making a calculation.

Taking it further

Students who demonstrate a thorough understanding of the process of calculating missing sides can consider how to calculate the angles in a right-angled triangle if they provide each other with the length of the hypotenuse and one of the two remaining sides. This means students will need to consider an inverse process involving the use of either the $\sin^{-1}$ or $\cos^{-1}$ functions.

Clearly students have effectively produced (measured) values for cosine and sine tables, and one important aspect of the continuing work is the procedure by which they have created cos and sin tables. However, they do not need to know these facts because they are about to be revealed!

Ask students to add two extra columns to their tables; one for cos and one for sin. Explain how to calculate cos and sin on a calculator, and ask the students to do this for each angle and fill in the new columns for the angles from 0° to 90°, to two decimal places. Depending upon the accuracy of their measuring, drawing and estimating from the initial task they should find these new results remarkably similar.

At this point it would be worth holding a whole-class discussion about what cos and sin could mean.

The next stage is for students to return to their rotating arm sheet and drop some verticals from the end-points of positions of the rotating arm. This will show that what they have produced is be a set of right-angled triangles with one measured angle.

Students can then continue to check the cos and sin values for the other angles they measured in *Circular functions I*.

From this point on students are to 'think' right-angled triangles when asked to carry out a calculation. Students need to understand that the rotating arm will be called the hypotenuse, which is the longest side in a right-angled triangle, and the other two sides will be referred to as the side 'opposite' the given angle and the side 'adjacent' to the given angle.

Ask students to calculate the lengths of the missing sides for these right-angled triangles.

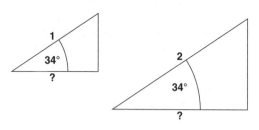

The crux issue here is that of enlargement and similar triangles. The calculator sequences for the two situations will be cos 34 × 1 = and cos 34 × 1 =.

Students now need plenty of practise of working out missing sides by writing the associated calculator sequences. One way to achieve this is for students to work in pairs as follows.

- Each student draws some life size diagrams, measures an angle and all three sides.
- Students give their partner a scale drawing showing the angle and the length of the hypotenuse and asks them to work out the other two missing sides.
- All answers should be written to an accuracy of one decimal place.
- Students then check each other's calculations against the previously measured sides.

Shapes in a square

"Changing simple conditions can lead to complex problems!"

This idea combines several mathematical skills and begins by considering some shapes made by joining mid-points and corners of a square.

Ask students to identify the mid-points of the edges on a square piece of paper. Then tell them to mark two straight lines on the paper. The rules are that they can join mid-points to mid-points, corners to corners or mid-points to corners. The lines may or may not meet, but they must not intersect.

The lines will split the square into a number of new shapes. Can the students calculate the area of each internal shape if the area of the whole square is 1? How many different diagrams can be produced and what are the areas of the shapes so produced?

Most diagrams produce relatively easy areas to calculate and this is a starting point for more challenging situations.

Sequences, functions and graphs

Part 6

Summing linear sequences

"I am always surprised that summing sequences is something that does not get much attention until KS4, with a proof of the formulae emerging at KS5."

This idea builds up the concept of the summation of linear sequences, making it accessible to KS3 students.

Ask students to write lists of five consecutive numbers within the range 1 to 20 and add the numbers. For example, the sequence 4, 5, 6, 7, 8 sums to 30 and the sequence 7, 8, 9, 10, 11 sums to 45. Gather a selection of students' data and ask them to discuss in pairs the different ways they can calculate the sums without adding each value one-by-one.

Gathering different responses will enable students to recognise that something is 'going on'. Will they come up with the notion of the answer always being the middle value multiplied by 5?

What happens for sequences of six, seven or three consecutive numbers?

Ask students to think about how they might write a statement to describe how to calculate the sum of a sequence of consecutive numbers given the first and the last numbers and the number of numbers. What happens if negative numbers are allowed?

Backwards sequences

"Looking for patterns is at the heart of mathematics."

There are many instances of exercises where students are either asked to fill in missing numbers or extend a sequence by a given number of terms. An extension of this is to extend sequences backwards and see what the graph looks like.

Extending linear sequences backwards provides a context for students to work with negative numbers. For example by extending the sequence 4, 7, 10, 13, 16 backwards by five terms we gain: −11, −8, −5, −2, 1, 4, 7, 10, 13, 16.

To graph these results, the terms 4, 7, 10, 13, 16 need to be associated with the term numbers 1, 2, 3, 4 and 5. Going backwards can be thought of as completing the table:

−4	−3	−2	−1	0	1	2	3	4	5
					4	7	10	13	16

Extending a quadratic sequence backwards will illustrate the symmetry involved. For example taking the quadratic sequence 1, 3, 6, 10, 15 backwards by five terms produces 10, 6, 3, 1, 0, 1, 3, 6, 10, 15.

Extending the Fibonacci sequence, 1, 1, 2, 3, 5, 8 backwards by lots of terms produces a most interesting oscillating pattern.

What happens when the numbers 1, 3, 4, 7, 11 from the Lucas sequence are extended backwards?

What happens when a power sequence is extended backwards? For example: 1, 3, 9, 27, 81.

Teaching tip

To extend the Fibonacci and Lucas sequences backwards, start by subtracting the first term from the second term to produce a new first term, then repeat with the new first and second terms.

Taking it further

Suppose a sequence is based upon two values *a* and *b* where the next value in the sequence is created by calculating $2a + b$. A sequence starting with 2 and 3 creates the following: 2, 3, 7, 13, 27, 53 . . . What happens when this sequence is reversed?

IDEA 97

Graphing factor pairs

"Finding opportunities for students to see concepts emerge in different contexts and to see how concepts are connected together in different ways is necessary if mathematics is to be perceived as a coherent discipline."

This idea is initially aimed at the lower KS3 age range and requires students to have access to a simple (non-scientific) calculator. The idea connects the concepts of factors and drawing graphs.

Teaching tip

Hold a discussion about what the students see when they look at the graph, to touch upon the ideas that the graph will never actually meet either the x- or y-axes, and that the graph is symmetrical about the line $y = x$.

Taking it further

When are the two dimensions equal? This question is aimed at students making sense of the concept of a square root, particularly if different degrees of accuracy are searched for prior to directing any of the students to the existence of the square root key on a calculator.

Ask students to write the pairs of factors of 24 as co-ordinate pairs, i.e. (1, 24), (2, 12), (3, 8), (4, 6), (6, 4), (8, 3), (12, 2) and (24, 1).

Instruct students to plot these points on a graph and join them together with a smooth curve. This is effectively drawing a graph of $y = 24/x$.

Extend the task by asking students to consider values that are not divisors of 24, such as 5, 7 or 9. By examining the graph to see what the missing ordinate is in the co-ordinate pair (5, ?), (7, ?), students can see how accurate, or otherwise, their readings are. Once the missing ordinates have been found, within a degree of accuracy provided by the graph, students can check how close they are using both multiplication [5 x 4.8 = 24] and division [24 ÷ 5 = 4.8]. Enabling students to recognise inverse operations at work will enhance a key mathematical process.

Students will have departed from working with whole number solutions at this point. However, the key issue is that all the points between whole number co-ordinate pairs continue to have points on the graph.

Students can explore the shape of other graphs by considering factor pairs for other numbers such as 30 and 20.

Quadratics I

"Working in ways so students become engaged with concepts such as algebra, quadratics etc is one way of preventing the question: 'What use will this be when I leave school?'"

This is a practise and consolidation type idea to help students become confident with the mechanics of multiplying out expressions in pairs of brackets.

This idea will help students practise and consolidate the skill of multiplying out pairs of expressions.

Provide students with sheets of A3 or sugar paper. Ask them to draw a line down the middle of their sheet (portrait orientation) and write their name at the top of each half.

On the left-hand side of the line students should write a number of pairs of factorised expressions, for example, $(x + 2)(x + 5)$. Using whatever methods they know, students should then work out the expansion of each expression, for example, $x^2 + 7x + 10$, and write this on the other side of the line. Suggest that they start with easy expressions of the form $(x + a)(x + b)$ and gradually write harder ones introducing negative terms and coefficients of x that are greater than 1.

Once students have several factorised expressions on the left-hand side of their paper and the equivalent expansions on the right-hand side, tell them to cut their sheet down the dividing line and swap their expanded expressions with another student. They now have to work out the factorisations for each other's expressions, and can subsequently check their answers with one another.

Teaching tip

Teachers will have different ways of explaining the process of multiplying out brackets. One approach is to use a two-way grid method, as used for multiplying numbers greater than 10 together.

Taking it further

The most confident students could try to expand three sets of factors to produce cubic expressions, for example, $(x + a)(x + b)(x + c)$.

Quadratics II

"Graphical calculators and function graph plotting computer programs are marvellous tools to aid learning, but I also want students to experience graphs by drawing them from first principles."

This idea is based upon students exploring a range of connected functions, which all have a coefficient of 1 for the x^2 term. The first task is for students to work in pairs to produce some display materials which will, in turn, act as a stimulus for discussion.

Teaching tip

It does not matter if some pairs of students do more than others as this is one aspect of differentiated learning. What is important is gathering together enough information to form an instant display.

Provide pairs of students with an A3 sheet of square grid paper showing a pair of axes and the function $f(x) = x^2$ drawn in thick felt tip.

Ask them to plot the following graphs, each on a separate sheet of paper.

- $f(x) = x^2 + 2$
- $f(x) = x^2 - 2$
- $f(x) = (x + 2)^2$
- $f(x) = (x - 2)^2$
- $f(x) = (x + 2)^2 + 2$
- $f(x) = (x + 2)^2 - 2$
- $f(x) = (x - 2)^2 + 2$
- $f(x) = (x - 2)^2 - 2.$

Because the coefficient of the x^2 term is always 1, each graph will obviously have the same shape but will be positioned differently on the grid.

Taking it further

A further development is for students to predict what happens if the graph is $y = x^2 + 3$ or $y = (x - 3)^2$ etc. Seeing what happens when the coefficient of the x^2 term becomes -1 will provide students with plenty to think about and try to make sense of. They can also classify graphs in terms of whether they have two, one or no real roots.

Other valuable information, in terms of analysing the graphs, is where the line of symmetry is; again this information can be connected to the function under discussion.

Discussing how each of the graphs is a vector translation of $y = x^2$ is a development of this work, and determining how the vector translation relates to the corresponding function is a further complexity.

Quadratics III

"One of the great pleasures of learning mathematics is for students to see how new ideas are constructed upon those they already know about."

This idea is a development from *Quadratics I* and *II*. These ideas, together with further work on completing the square and deriving the traditional formula for solving a quadratic, can form the basis for a unit lasting a minimum of three weeks.

Having considered quadratics when the coefficient of the x^2 term is 1, this idea will develop students' thinking by considering coefficients of the x^2 term as something other than 1. Follow the same procedure as described in *Quadratics II*; students could even reuse the paper with the $y = x^2$ graph already drawn on it.

Some options for graphs to draw are:

- $y = 2x^2$
- $y = 2x^2 - 3$
- $y = 2x^2 + 3$
- $y = 2x^2 + x - 3$
- $y = 2x^2 + x + 3$
- $y = 2x^2 - x - 3$
- $y = 2x^2 - x + 3$
- $y = \frac{1}{2}x^2$
- $y = \frac{1}{2}x^2 - 3$
- $y = \frac{1}{2}x^2 + 3$
- $y = \frac{1}{2}x^2 + x - 3$
- $y = \frac{1}{2}x^2 + x + 3$ etc.

Once students have produced enough graphs to form a display they can again gather around their work to discuss and analyse similarities and differences. The key aspects of this task are to recognise how the graphs compare to each other and to $y = x^2$ and to explore the real roots and the turning point for quadratics of the form: $y = ax^2 + bx + c$ where a, b and c are in the range -4 to 4.

Teaching tip

Encourage the use of graphical calculators or a graph plotting program to help students start to examine what the real roots are, if any exist, together with the turning points of graphs of quadratic functions. These tools will also allow students to systematically gather a lot of information for purposes of analysis.

Taking it further

The most confident students might be able to construct a procedure for predicting whether a function will have two, one or no real roots and where these real roots are, and some are likely to be capable of constructing a procedure for determining the turning point.